A Chef in Provence
with Édouard Loubet

To my loved ones, family and friends.
To my teachers, who taught me to be rigorous and to value a job well done.

Notes

1. Standard level spoon measurements are used in all recipes.
   1 tablespoon = one 15 ml spoon; 1 teaspoon = one 5 ml spoon
2. Both imperial and metric measurements have been given in all recipes.
   Use one set of measurements only and not a mixture of both.
3. Eggs should be medium unless otherwise stated. It is prudent for more
   vulnerable people to avoid uncooked or lightly cooked dishes made with eggs.
   Once prepared, these dishes should be kept in the refrigerator and used promptly.
4. Milk should be full fat unless otherwise stated.
5. Fresh herbs should be used unless otherwise stated.
6. Ovens should be preheated to the specified temperature.
7. Pepper should be freshly ground black pepper unless otherwise stated.
8. Some recipes contain nuts and nut derivatives.

The team would like to dedicate this book to the gourmet editor and
food lover Pierre Marchand.

Editor
Brigitte Éveno, assisted by Carole Vernis

Design
Dune Lunel/Modzilla

Editorial secretary
Anne Fitament-Peter

Proofreading
Chloé Chauveau & Sophie Brissaud

Production
Felicity O'Connor

Photoengraving: APS Chromostyle

First published by Hachette Pratique, an imprint of Hachette Livre
43 Quai de Grenelle, Paris 75905, Cedex 15, France
Under the title *Un printemps en Luberon*
© 2002, Hachette Livre (Hachette Pratique)
All rights reserved

English language translation produced by Tess Holly Drage and Erica Stenfalt
for Translate-A-Book, Oxford

This edition published by Hachette Illustrated UK, Octopus Publishing Group,
2–4 Heron Quays, London, E14 4JP
© 2004 English Translation, Octopus Publishing Group Ltd, London

Printed by Tien Wah, Singapore
ISBN: 1-84430-053-6

A Chef in Provence
with Édouard Loubet

80 recipes from the Moulin at Lourmarin
Preface by Peter Mayle

Photographs by **Jacques Guillard**
With the editorial contribution of **Catherine Vialard**

Preface by Peter Mayle

The chef with his harvest
As in nature, there is always something to pick in the kitchen garden.

Last year, for my birthday, my wife presented me with a puppy: a pedigree Griffon Korthals, shaggy, golden-eyed, and equipped with a telepathic ability that can sense the presence of a bird hidden in a bush twenty metres away. We named the pup Nellie.

She was only eight weeks old when she met her first Michelin-starred chef: Édouard Loubet had stopped at the house on his way into the wilds of the Luberon, and the two of them – man and puppy – were introduced. Édouard had a *coup de foudre*. He was enchanted. And, being a hunter, he recognized the breed. Where had we found her?

We told him that Nellie had been born in Marseille, accompanied by ten brothers and sisters. If he was interested, there was a chance that one might still be available. Édouard made a call, rushed down to Marseille, and drove back with a hairy passenger, Nellie's brother Scott. A year passed before brother and sister met one another, and the difference between them was startling. Édouard's

dog was a magnificent specimen – enormous – half as big again as ours. And yet they had been born on the same day, to the same mother.

it is, of course, quite normal that the male is slightly bigger than the female, but my suspicion is that something other than genes is at work here. Its diet; or perhaps I should say cuisine. A chef's dog eats well – in the case of this chef, extremely well.

My wife and I have spent many contented hours at Le Moulin, but there is one particular occasion that will always stay in that part of my memory where the best souvenirs are kept.

it was our first Christmas in a house we were sharing with the masons, electricians, plumbers and painters that seem to be recurring figures in our lives. That cold December, the house was a work in progress, the kitchen not much more than a gleam in the architect's eye. It showed promise, but it was certainly not a room to inspire the cooking of a festive meal. And so we decided to leave the dust and the dangling electrical wires behind, go to Le Moulin, and treat ourselves to Édouard's Christmas lunch menu.

It was about half past twelve when we sat down at our table in the vast stone room, warmed by a log fire in the hearth, surrounded by the encouraging sounds and smells that combine to make an aperitif for the senses: the muted creak of corks being eased out of bottles, the perfumed zephyrs coming from a passing bowl of *ragout d'escargots* and a basket of warm bread, the murmured recitations of the sommelier. Anticipation, that most potent stimulus to healthy appetites, was in the air. Bring on the first course!

But no. Before letting his clients start on the serious business of the menu, it is Édouard's pleasant habit to give them, as a kind of gastronomic warm-up, a preliminary dish (or two) to set the scene for the pleasures to come. They are no more than a couple of mouthfuls, just enough to rouse the taste buds, but they are presented and served with all the ceremony and attention to detail due to a main course.

In fact, we were given two of these miniature works of art, followed by the first course, followed by the main course, followed by a 'Pause Provençale' to allow us to catch our breath, followed by cheeses, followed by an *avant-dessert*, followed by dessert, followed by coffee (accompanied, of course, by an assortment of *mignardises* in case we were feeling deprived). A worthy gift for the Christmas stomach.

It was a wonderful meal in many ways. Édouard's cooking is well known for its inventiveness and its inspired use of herbs, the sometimes unlikely but always successful combinations of flavours and textures, the 'surprises in the mouth'. Beyond that, however, there were three other things that struck us about that lunch.

The generosity of the menu was quite extraordinary; not in terms of bulk, but in the variety of tastes that succeeded one another. Never overpowering or deadening to the appetite, they took the palate on a tour of discovery without a single false step.

And it was light, all of it. Even though, when we added them up, we realized we had made our way through seven different courses of varying sizes, there was no feeling of having eaten too much. Satisfaction without surfeit is not an easy balance to achieve, and it takes a master chef to achieve it.

The final memory concerns time. We left the restaurant to discover that the afternoon had somehow disappeared. The lights of Lourmarin were on, and winter darkness was setting in. We had spent four and a half hours at the table, and it didn't seem a minute too long.

Although I can't think of a more pleasant way to pass four and a half hours, such extended indulgence is not always possible. Real life intervenes. Work has to be finished. Appointments have to be kept. Dogs have to be walked. Chores have to be done. There are times when these demands make a Christmas-length lunch out of the question.

When this happens, we have learned that it is best to warn the chef in advance, in case he has another seven-course treat up his sleeve. Experience has taught us that we need to be firm, and the following exchange is fairly typical:

'Édouard, we only have two hours, maybe two and a half. We must be out of here before three o'clock.'

The Loubet eyebrows are raised at the thought of such indecent haste. 'Ah bon?' he says, 'Well, I'll see what I can do.'

And he does. And it's delicious.

Peter Mayle, July 2002

Peter Mayle and Édouard
with Nellie and Scott,
the two griffons.

Contents

Left:
Édouard Loubet
gathers rocket flowers near Lourmarin –
demonstrating just one aspect of a highly
complex personality.

A Chef in Provence
with Édouard Loubet

The hills of the Luberon inspire profound thoughts. They welcome all who truly understand them. Édouard Loubet has crossed them path by path. The stone and gravel tracks and the rocky outcrops cutting through the vegetation, have spilled their secrets to him. From them he gathers cold bare stones, first sharpened into flints by the earliest settlers, and then he arranges them like a jigsaw *en calades* – a Provençal style of paving. He is Master of the Mourre Nègre, highest peak in the Luberon, and a mountain biker's dream. Set like a giant tooth, the village of Saignon, a blaze of lavender, stands out on the horizon. One's gaze lands on the rock faces; in summer they will turn green, dotted with all manner of herbs. Soon the ground will be a carpet of aromatic herbs and flowers where sheep will be free to graze. The hills seem almost to indulge in a weary indolence. They are in no hurry, like silkworms in metamorphosis, which leave the nourishing sap and warmth of the silken cocoons where they have spent the winter, only to bury themselves and grow into chrysalises. By the time they emerge as butterflies, the hillside will be unrecognizable. Already the spring grass is scattered with patches of violets, bushes of fuchsia and wild thyme. Along from them the crocuses are just coming into bloom. Their sweet flavoured pollen will stain the palate saffron yellow. Here and there, the hare and the wild boar, rulers of the slopes, dig into the ground. A shepherd's hut exposed to the winds and a nesting box remind us that people live here. This is Marcel Pagnol and Jean Giono country, home of *Manon des Sources* and *Hussard sur le Toit*.

Above:
On the horizon,
the peaks of the Luberon, where
the light is forever changing.

A mountain in spring

Spring is not just about the radiant light of Cézanne's Provence; there are the grey-blue skies, the raindrops falling from the branches of cherry trees in bud and the smoke of wood fires dancing from the chimneys. Sometimes this mountain will offer comfort, at other times sadness. Édouard knows all its moods well. He could happily live here like a latter-day Robinson Crusoe, hidden away from everyone in a hut high among the trees, combing the land for fresh peas and wild cherries, spring asparagus and salsify and liquorice roots. This former skier left the white slopes of Savoie for the verdant richness of this 1,100-metre (3,600-foot) mountain, settling in a hamlet voted the *plus beau village de France* – the most beautiful village in France. Lourmarin nestles in the small valley separating the Grand Luberon from the Petit Luberon, a reminder of the Mediterranean's frenzied activity during the Tertiary period: its waters tore into the land splitting it into two islands. As if blessed by the gods, this village of enchanting beauty with its thousand inhabitants has been spared from the surge of property development that has swept across the Côte d'Azur. Artists come here to capture the colours of spring; writers, following the example of Camus and Bosco, find their inspiration here. There are those who visit as pilgrims to meditate at Camus' grave; while others return to the village for the cuisine of its ancient olive oil mill, situated at the foot of the Renaissance castle – which now houses an institute of art.

The birth of the Moulin

Spring prompts the rebirth of Nature; the Moulin also opened in spring. Early in March, the very first guests, as yet intrigued, walked in under an archway lit up with a blaze of sunflowers; this alone showed the Maître of the house to be an original. The fact is, things were not easy to begin with. Few, if any, believed in this young man down from the mountains, charging headlong into a business that had already failed twice. Provence was not about to welcome with open arms this ambitious youngster and, what's more, a Savoyard. It took a while for the locals to admit that the driving force of his energetic imagination was nothing less than a quest for perfection.

Still in its early stages, the Moulin is suddenly an irrepressible hive of activity. All of the 18 rooms are taken and the dining room is full. A century-old olive tree, transplanted in the garden on the owner's impulse, quietly reflects on this commotion.

Inside, nature seems to permeate each detail: the freshly pressed linen of the staff's outfits, the walls in eggshell coloured stone or lined in polished lambskin, the big wicker linen baskets – some filled with herbs, others with squash and marrow – serving as coffee tables, the massive 80 kg (176 lb) pumpkin carved with the Moulin's name on its side, the magnificent sheaves of wild oats adorning the entrance... The figure of an Amazon warrior dominates the reception desk. She is 'Semeuse', all wrought iron and straw, arms outstretched like branches – born of Édouard's vivid imagination. We are in a world of fine fabrics, wrought iron, stone and wood; at the very heart of French craftsmanship and of an appreciation of the beauty of natural materials. The Moulin, bright and spacious, offers plenty of room to wander about. The glass lift takes you to the first floor; from there it is back down a few steps to the bar, which in turn

Édouard's restaurant,
situated in an ancient olive oil mill, is tucked away in Lourmarin, one of the *plus beaux villages de France*.

overlooks the dining room. The oversized squared plates in midnight blue by Terre de Provence soften the radiant yellow of the tablecloths. Pots of different jam, such as apricot or green tomato like our grandmothers used to make, are neatly lined up along the picture window or tucked into the little recesses of the alcoves. Off in a corner, away from the rest, a straw-coloured marrow stands by a bouquet of dried flowers – a memory of the summer's harvest. The arch of the light and airy vaulted ceiling reaches down to what remains of the centuries-old olive oil mill – an impressive wooden structure now heavily eroded with time.

Discreet lighting pours an iridescent glow on to the tables decorated with sprigs of almond flowers. Touches of herbs and hyssop petals sit on a dusting of flour or ground hazelnuts. The light begins to fade and nothing in the world could draw one away from the vaulted dining room. The ancient mill was back with a vengeance and has worked at full speed ever since. Today, one of the region's top restaurants, recognized by the highly selective *Guide Michelin*, the Moulin de Lourmarin no longer stands empty.

To achieve so resounding a success, the young chef was forced to complete his very own 'twelve labours of Hercules'. He had to master two new environments; one, the world of the restaurateur, the other, life in Provence. Not so easy for one who still longed for the snow-covered slopes back home, where he was once champion of the French junior team for the Comité de Savoie.

There he was confined to a kitchen behind hot stoves, he of all people, whose only dreams were of wide-open spaces and the fresh mountain air. His mother however, could breath easy. Phew! Her madcap son was finally settled down. François Prudent, Édouard's stepfather, had made the young tearaway see sense. 'Skiing, far too risky! Cooking on the other hand...' The fearless young man had the wisdom to follow the advice of his various spiritual mentors, his stepfather, his skiing instructors, Dominique Tournier and Michel Folier, and later on the chefs Alain Chapel and Marc Veyrat. But on one condition: he was to be the best.

As for his freedom – he rediscovered it in his beloved Luberon, where he was now well known for his somewhat self-willed, carefree attitude. In the kitchen he re-creates Nature's fragrances and aromas when he simmers a bunch of wild thyme or roasts a rack of lamb. Édouard can sense the sun all around him; in a sunflower – his personal emblem – or in the flower of a simple Jerusalem artichoke.

Finally, with a new-found sense of belonging, he knows where he is heading. Hidden under his wide-brimmed hat he sets off, like a solitary hunter, to check if that crocus which this morning was barely open...

The spirit of a champion, the will of a pioneer

The press was swift to recognize the talent of the young chef. News spread that he had set up at the Moulin in 1993; soon after, in 1996, he secured his first Michelin star. Going back just for a moment – still a mere toddler, he was already playing with pots and pans under the watchful eye of his grandmother, Raymonde. Add to this his grandad Yvon, a gardener, parents who owned a restaurant, and you have the makings of a chef.

Now France's top apprentice, he took off, and together with Fernand Guterez, headed for the Ritz-Carlton, taking on the challenge of a tough American organization. Barely out of his teens, he wrote to the 20 finest chefs in the country. Just one answered, but by no means the least. Alain Chapel invited him to Mionnay, but it was the celebrated Savoyard Marc Veyrat who was to influence him the most. Next to these two masters, Édouard learned that technique alone is not enough; what one needs is intuition and sensitivity. And suddenly there he was at 24, the youngest Michelin-starred chef in France. 'I had given

myself five years. I never thought this would happen so fast. I cried with joy, excitement and surprise.' This distinction in no way weakened his determination, which was duly rewarded with a second star three years later.

'Édouard Loubet, rising star of the Luberon', 'A dazzling career path' (Two stars in six years), 'Cuisine's child prodigy', 'France's youngest

starred chef", 'The Moulin of the stars': the press had a complete field day lavishing on him rhapsodic praise, extolling the tour de force of the *gavroche des alpages* – the little urchin of the alpine slopes. Édouard is of pioneer stock. His grandfather, realizing he could no longer make a living from mountain farming had already transformed himself into a restaurant owner in the late 1960s, opening 'Le Glouglou' in Val Thorens – a workman's eatery specializing in pastries and tarts, of which his mother, a

former hair stylist, persevered in her conquest as a charismatic businesswoman. 'A Relais et Chateaux in Val Tho? Impossible, no chance!' However, impossible is not the Loubet way. From there the Loubet clan resurrected the Moulin: Édouard's mother responsible for reception and finance, his grandfather in the garden and his grandmother in charge of jam making. Two years on and the wheels of the Moulin were turning of their own accord, the family withdrew, leaving Édouard sole master.

Above:
Yvon Loubet,
his grandfather and the
family's first restaurateur.

A man imbued with **tradition**

'The Savoyards are steeped in their traditions. I discovered this same affinity in the people of Provence, as is even evident from such details

abrupt, harsh character, while outwardly appearing far more gentle, thanks to a warm, friendly disposition. This was, at times, to cost me disappointment and let down. In Savoie it is time and friendship – nothing else – which open doors, but once open, they stay that way. In Provence however, all doors are open – to allow the Mistral free passage. It was not easy for me to understand this contrast between mountain severity and the energy and conviviality of the south. Yet when I see the people here going about their work, be it tending their asparagus or their carrots, or in among the hay, I recognize my same fundamental principle – a respect for nature.' Among the herbs of the Luberon Édouard also discovered the flavours and aromas of alpine pastures; he had to temper and soften them as the force of the Mistral tends to make them more intense and unpredictable.

'I am an observer,' Édouard tells us. 'On my days off, while working for M. Chapel, I would visit the Lyonnais chef Pierre Orsi. I would observe and take in what I saw: people's gestures, mannerisms, moods and traditions. That's why I love to meet up with the old folk who always have something to teach me. Older people have a beauty all their

Above:
Two men of the soil,
Adrien Lombard the gardener
(left), and Paul Davin, Lourmarin
farmer (right), both loyal allies
of Édouard.

as the signposts when you enter a village written in both French and Provençal, or the radio broadcasting programmes in the local dialect. I also found that they share the same own, they have such presence.' It was from them that Édouard learned how to prune a vine or straighten a crooked nail; they told him about the origins of traditional festivities and of the struggles between the monasteries and the churches of a Protestant stronghold torn apart by the wars of religion...

Catch him at his home, the Petit Moulin, outside the old sheep pen he uses for smoking his haunch of venison, musing over an orange juice into which he dips his *pain au chocolat*: you could take him for a peasant. Indeed, he has plenty of good old-fashioned acumen for not wasting resources. Édouard transforms vegetables which we normally discard into the most magnificent sauces. Two crates of trimmings for one of cleaned asparagus? He is quick to spot a good deal and sets about finding use for this tangled mass of greenery. 'I would love to have been born just after the War, when times were hard and people simply had to manage somehow. I would have traded walnuts for butter...'

As a child of Nature and of tradition, Édouard is superstitious. In both pockets he carries an *oeil de Sainte-Lucie* (the eye of St. Lucy – patron saint of the people of Marseille), a good luck seashell sold in the port of Marseille.

Is it mere coincidence that a man of tradition now finds himself in one of the region's ancient mills, so prosperous during the nineteenth century? But, interestingly, this particular man – a mass of contradictions – is anything but traditional in the kitchen.

Between **memory** and **flair** – a **master** fulfilled

Even Édouard's friends find it difficult to understand such a gift for succeeding at every turn. 'You don't have a clue in the garden, you never go by the rules, yet you still achieve magnificent results! Dogs, horses, even aubergines, do your bidding,' moans Adrien, the gardener.

His secret lies hidden somewhere between recollection and spontaneity. His creativeness draws on the authentic. This Michelin-starred chef has in no way renounced the food-loving little boy he once was. Witness the superb *gratin de ma grand-mère* (a deliciously smooth potato gratin), or the *denti à la fleur de sel* (wild sea bream in a salt crust – a childhood memory of the Corsican coast). 'I have the utmost respect for those flavours which linger in someone's memory after eating a particular food. A sauce of oregano and beetroot served as accompaniment to lamb's liver will, in turn, develop its own flavour of liver.' One taste can bring in another. The slight hint of earthiness typical of both sage and sea bass is refined in a dish with hints of orange. Édouard likes to explore flavours from far and wide: for example, the aromas of *sangria* which he reinvents in a *papillote croustillante de gibier au chocolat accompagnée de chips d'orange* (a game parcel with a chocolate sauce, served with a zest of orange crisp.)

Naturally, Édouard has great regard for other people's memories of tastes but he goes beyond them. As he explores, redefining true, authentic flavours, we overcome any instinctive reservations we may have. Our memory, rather like a distorting mirror, can make a false connection between smell and taste, or between a tender consistency and a delicate flavour. Thus, an asparagus *bouillon* which may seem too salty, is somewhat stronger and sharper because it has been prepared using the trimmings. 'The true

flavour. Savory, for example, has a feminine and fruity smell with a hint of orange which on the palate is sharp, acidic, even peppery. Always ready for a challenge, Édouard also enjoys opposing this. 'With some dishes, notably those involving any strong scent, such as jasmine, marjoram or wild celery, I try to reproduce the fragrance of a plant, taking my cue from its most dominant aroma.'

As for spontaneity? It comes in part from his fascination with obscure ingredients – long-forgotten vegetables, spices from Puerto Rico... But it is also his passion for inventing a dish on the spot with no opportunity to practise, much to the frenzy of his staff. 'Each new creation of mine is born from an idea which I gradually develop in my mind and also from a strong intuitive feeling. Rarely am I happy with the initial attempt. The moment of inspiration tends to come in the middle of the service – I find myself reverting to the idea I had in its original form, now rid of whatever added flavours I might have been tempted to include.' Instinctively, he knows simplicity approaches the sublime.

Above all, Édouard understands 'the spontaneity inherent in the language of Nature' – his principle source of inspiration. He gathers and draws from the very essence of the Luberon, reinterpreting it in a cuisine free of all convention. When he serves a vegetable as a dessert, for example, it is not out of a desire to be original or fashionable. As long as he likes a flavour, and it works, it makes sense to him – whether a soup of wild strawberries with a celery sorbet or a carrot salad served with a wine granita. His flavours will invariably complement one another.

Skilful and inspirational, audacious or untutored, Édouard's cuisine cannot be defined; where infusion meets blending, flexibility mixes with the most exacting precision, instinct mingles with perception.

In the expert hands of the chef, herbs release new aromas.

flavour of vegetables lies in their skin.' Our memory of a fragrance can be misleading and can hinder and impair the tasting process. Some clients do not fully appreciate his *crème brûlée à la lavande* because in their minds lavender is synonymous with soap. Similarly, doctors tend to avoid his *glace à l'eucalyptus*, as to them it suggests a medicinal flavour. Fortunately, with the exception of lavender, rosemary, narcissus and jonquil, few herbs or flowers have a taste resembling their smell. Indeed, a plant's scent often hides a different

An artistic chef

Édouard will dream of a dish before actually preparing it. As he goes walking in his beloved Luberon, he draws in his mind every feature and flavour, trying to sense which herbs might best enhance it. Then he tries it out . 'Very Gagnaire!' remarks his chef Alex cheekily. Édouard builds the dish into the shape of a pyramid, adding an elegant touch with the juice of pressed herbs. 'It's Ducasse now!' now annoyed, he replaces the deep plate with a flat one. He's got it! He is an artistic chef, not a chef-cum-artist. He uses ingredients as he would colour – vivid, conflicting shades, striking but still in harmony. So it is with words. Just to hear him speak of the hills so dear to him... the titles of his recipes each tell a story – the spattering butter, the bubbling sauce... Like a prologue to the tastes ahead, these gourmet headings seem almost to nourish us as we await the arrival of a dish.

A disaster at school, a winner on the slopes, with a talent for impudence; he is chef, designer and inventor – a true artist. 'I would have loved to have worked with wrought iron but most of all to have gone into carpentry – working with form and design in three dimensions. I adore the smell of fresh wood and the action of the lathe cutting into it at full speed. In the kitchen too, I like to work with shapes and use the visual aspect to best advantage. I might draw a square on a round dish for instance.' To begin with Édouard chose to work in *pâtisserie*, involving him in the aesthetic side of cuisine. However, the rigours of this training with its exacting precision and fixed recipes soon put him off. 'In all other cuisine I am free to boil, to simmer, to sauté, to improvise.' Herein we see what lies at the very heart of his work – an explosive mix of the intuitiveness of an artist together with the energy of a man of unstoppable drive.

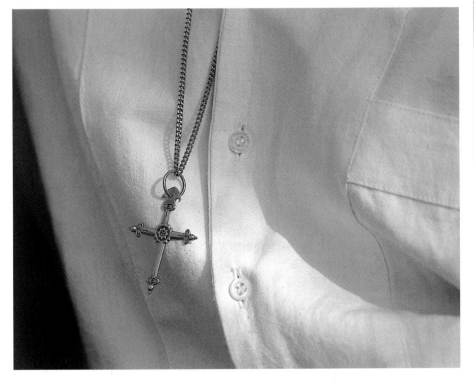

Right:
No dessert without an
avant-dessert –
Carottes râpées a l'anis et
granité de vin jaune

A daredevil in the kitchen

Rock climbing, diving, sailing, water-skiing, motorcycling, underwater fishing, you name it – with the possible exception of cricket, Édouard has done the lot. In the kitchen, he displays this same non-conformist quality offering dishes where fresh, vigorous aromas meet in striking contrast. This madcap has in no way lost his taste for risk-taking; who else would dare to serve snails with a *tabac* of wild herbs from the Luberon, or pike-perch poached in a *jus* of catmint. Those who believe that harmony of flavour is paramount would consider this an outrage. But this apparent assault on the palate is not without great sensitivity and consideration. So too the eloquent, vivid description of a dish presented by a true master, timed to accompany the moment of its arrival and carried by an earnest young man straight out of the eighteenth century. At this point the sommelier goes way beyond the rapport between food and wine. 'Take my advice, you should mix the *granité de vin jaune* with the carrots, then bite into the *anis* biscuit.

I remember first trying it, I immediately thought of a Coteaux-du-Layon, which is excellent with the refreshing hint of acidity in the dish. Well, what's your verdict?' Nothing but praise, monsieur Charly! Like Édouard, Charly dismisses all clichés. 'Red wine with cheese – a big mistake. The bacteria mask the tannins and impair the sharpness. You would do better with a white, preferably from the same region as the cheese; for example, a Luberon Constantin Chevalier with a banon.' Remarkably audacious, the food here leaves no room for any distraction such as light conversation or, worse still, business talk. You cannot avoid pondering on dishes such as snails hidden under a delicate green frothy sauce, purple sea urchin up against giant asparagus, or a crispy chocolate puff with a smooth centre grappling with a magnificent tuile. Everything is brimming with energy, bursting with vigour and of exceptional generosity. *Foie gras*, cut like pâté, sits on a thick slice of country bread. The menus offer a profusion of dishes; each one, however, has its place. In particular Édouard has reinvented the *entremets* – little in-between dishes which marked a pause during the extravagant banquets of the Middle Ages and which often went uneaten. Before a meat dish he offers a *bouillon* with a strong hint of vinegar to rouse the tastebuds. Pink grapefruit served with a eucalyptus ice cream or grated carrot served with a wine granita refresh the palate before the final delicacy, the dessert. Appetizers and *petits-fours* also have their place in the feast. This is too much! We're full! There are those who are wary of such abundance, rather like a gift they do not trust, and maybe some will not be back. What is surprising about this restaurant, offering such unconventional flavours, is that the clientele is for the most part local. They might well have been deterred by

the intensity of certain flavours and by this unrestrained inventiveness. However, they can tell the difference and have spotted the mark of his sincerity. Here, feeling replete does not destroy the desire to come back again.

Now an accredited chef, Édouard challenges the closed world of cuisine, throwing out new ideas. Thus, he won't draw his chickens any more than he will remove the stomach sac from a lobster. Often he won't peel his onions or garlic, but instead merely chops them into small pieces. And the result of all this... his cooking has flavour, real flavour. Guests first tasting a dish might find it too salty, too sharp or too... too what? Accustomed to more muted flavours, at first they are bewildered. Admittedly Édouard likes salt as an ingredient in its own right and will often present it separately on the plate as part of a dish. He listens and responds to any observation with the precision of a wine expert. He will talk through each individual flavour in a recipe and explain just why he has put them together. Here the parsnip brings a roundness to the dry fruitiness of wild cherry blossom, whereas here, the earthy flavours of Jerusalem artichoke are refined by the aroma of borage flower. In another dish, pine nuts enhance the smooth flavours of a rich and creamy soup. Nonetheless, behind these mild words lies the fiery energy of a man of many facets.

Harmony
of wine and food, and
between Charly the
sommelier and the chef.

The tempers of a Savoyard

Flying off the handle, arguing, fits of rage in part define the man they nickname 'Al Capone' – so calm when he goes walking in the hills. Take his chef for example; when the Moulin first opened it was very tough for him at work, even if away from it, they were really good buddies. One day, out of the blue, they had an argument and Alexandre stormed out. Immediately Édouard called him back. His outbursts are simply a part of his nature and are gone as quickly as they came. So it was when he fell out with Flavien, the butcher-baker of the Moulin, who dared get too friendly with Édouard's girlfriend. A *coup de boule* as they say in Provence, a 'quick step outside', and all is forgotten. Same story at l'Auberge de l'Eridan with Marc Veyrat, where once, in the middle of the service, after fighting like cats and dogs they parted company. Yet to this day they remain the very best of friends. 'Édouard has all the hallmarks of a master: talent, charisma and one hell of a temper,' Veyrat warns us. Such an impulsive nature works to his advantage. It is a guest's actual order which will galvanize him into finally perfecting a new dish – on the spot. 'If it's not right, I'll drop a recipe once and for all.' As with friendship, so too in cooking; after all the commotion comes reconciliation. 'At first I like to shock and surprise people, then I harmonize and balance the various flavours.'

A man of the soil who understands the language of herbs and stones

His bag, bursting with herbs of all kinds, on his shoulder, Édouard is back from another trek in the Luberon. His hair a mess, eyes gleaming, nostrils quivering with the fresh scents and his mind teaming with ideas for new recipes, there seems to be more of the hound than the man about him. But now returned to civilization, he reassumes his more familiar human form.

Nature itself is as dear to Édouard as his cuisine and he never separates one from the other. The land is not rich in wine alone; it brings the truffle, for example, gnawed at by field mice, or the cherry that the magpie likes to pick at. To him a truffle conjures up the picture of a plough and the freshly furrowed soil. Pine nuts evoke the image of the Provençal light, of a cypress or a pine cone. The thought of pigeon takes him straight to a field of rocket, just as lamb suggests the aroma of wild thyme. A countryman at heart, this great chef likes everything homemade, from bread to jam, to liqueurs even. Without nostalgia however; he is fully in touch with the times, the age of Coca-Cola cans and fast food. Here is a man who might have become a lumberjack, a geologist or carpenter. He is, in fact, hunter, herbalist and chef.

When he is not rooting around in the hills, you will find Édouard, boots covered in mud, in his garden: five hectares (12 acres) of herbs sown in strict rows: sage, lovage, wormwood, interspersed with sunflowers, poppies and burnet. He can identify the flavour of a herb at each stage of its life; the ones he loves best are those of a herb in flower, 'They are more delicate yet give maximum flavour'.

He likes to bite into a mushroom freshly plucked from the ground to capture its true taste; he will then focus on re-creating that same flavour on the plate. The warm and crispy exterior of his ceps in breadcrumbs explodes with the flavour of the raw mushroom within. 'If you have never tried a raw baby *oronge* (imperial mushroom) thinly sliced with a drop of hazelnut and walnut oil, and a touch of salt, you don't know what good food is,' declares the gardener Adrien, Édouard's partner in crime. His menu normally includes titles such as ragout of Jerusalem artichoke with truffle, toasted bread and earthy flavours. To Édouard, earth itself has a flavour in its own right and is not merely some abstract, remote concept. He is not just inspired by herbs – rinds, skins, leaves, petals and roots all matter. If it works, he will happily use a flavour no matter where he finds it; in a pine cone or even in trimmings if need be. Then like a *parfumier* he leaves it to settle by infusion, maceration, reduction...

A summary of Édouard's cuisine would have to include his love of herbs, which inspired him to settle in Provence – verbena, hyssop, wild thyme from the Claparèdes and New Zealand spinach. Then there are the flowers, among them his favourite the poppy, with its sharp-tasting stem giving off aromas of verbena and bergamot. His genius for herbs has restored the subtlety and good taste native to Provence; the region seemed to have renounced its charm and finesse, won over

instead by commercial success. Its distinctive character and creativity was lost, as shown by the worldwide proliferation of the tomato-basil-garlic trio. To those who cherish the Provence of old, of chefs Raymond Thuillier and Roger Vergé, Édouard's cuisine is like an invigorating fresh breeze sweeping across the region. Admittedly, he had to comply with the tradition of *anchoïade* as an appetizer. Mesclun, on the other hand, is no match for a salad which mixes delicate, tender hyssop with the vibrant purple of a forgotten variety of cabbage. Of equal importance in Provence is the truffle – white in summer, black in winter. Marseille is not far and Édouard often strolls through the port looking for a lesser-known type of fish or perhaps for sea urchins, notably the purple ones which look exquisite served with asparagus. A chef unlike any other, he seems to take the original flavours of his ingredients and sets them free. 'I absorb the very essence of my surroundings. If I lived by the sea, I would use sand, pebbles and seaweed for my sauces.'

But for now, Édouard grabs his hat, hanging from a nail in the kitchen, and with the jaunty gait of a mountain herdsman he sets off – spring will not wait. He keeps an eye out for the blossoming of the crocus and wild watercress, which bloom just before the thyme and lavender are in flower. Soon the crickets will be singing among the trees...

Left:
Rock and vegetation,
the world of the artist.

Top:
The Protestant church
opposite the chateau.

Above:
The school in Lourmarin,
once the home of
Philippe Girard, who invented
the linen spinning machine.

Adrien's garden —
the mill, water, land

Opposite:
Marjoram, rhubarb, mint,
rosemary and catnip
all grow in Édouard's garden.

Above:
Baby spinach shoots
are familiar with their
master's hand

Above right:
Basket of strawberries

Below right:
The sun rises
over Adrien and his garden

A mix of sweet scented bushes and rows of vegetables, Adrien's garden stands on the Lourmarin spring line, next to another abandoned mill, where Édouard has made his home. Adrien is an authority on plants; he knows all their secrets. He understands how best to combine certain types, such as Indian carnation with tomato and garlic, or white clover with leek. He is intrigued at how some plants die off prematurely as part of their natural evolution. To save the angelica, he will regularly trim its flowers when they bloom. No such worries with rocket however; it flowers as vigorously in the garden as in the vineyard. Adrien has all the enthusiasm of a child, 'Just look at my baby spinach shoots,' and the nonchalance of an adult, 'The spinach over there is nothing special'. He can be found on all fours scraping away at the earth, tearing at the couch grass with his bare hands. He keeps a close and watchful eye over the very first shoots: *radis gloriette* (a type of radish), beautifully plump and of a rich red colour, mint, lemon balm, lemon basil, cinnamon basil. Some come from afar, such as the strawberry spinach, a memory of Guyana. Broad beans he planted in November have already sprouted in February. Baby leeks sown very close together, hence their slender shape, will appear in April. Underground, the frilly lettuces are well on their way, whereas the verbena is only just beginning. Perennial herbs emerge from their winter torpor and burnet, having survived the early frosts, restarts its growth from the roots. It is time to sow marjoram, rue, the local herb *agastache* and savory – one of Édouard's favourites. And each week to re-sow the radishes and sunflowers.

The garden is just big enough. As soon as the chef goes off a particular plant, such as the winter cherry, Adrien gives up growing it. And already he is preparing the ground for the autumn plants, such as wormwood which returns with the thrushes.

Soups and savoury starters

Butternut squash soup with argan oil, almond blossom and toasted almonds • Chicken consommé with egg yolks and wild cherry blossom • Chilled Jerusalem artichoke, borage and rape flower soup • Mackerel pie with pigeon livers and 'old boy's jam' • Little snail stews with a 'tobacco' of Luberon herbs • Court-bouillon of baby turnips with seasonal truffles

Butternut squash soup with argan oil, almond blossom and toasted almonds

Serves 8
Preparation time: 30 minutes
Cooking time: 35 minutes

Ingredients:
50 g/2 oz flaked almonds
100 g/3½ oz butter

3 onions, finely chopped
50 g/2 oz pine nuts
1 kg/2 lb butternut squash, peeled, seeded and chopped
200 ml/7 fl oz white wine
1 litre/1¾ pints chicken stock (see page 184)
500 ml/18 fl oz milk
500 ml/18 fl oz single cream
1 handful parsley, leaves only
7 tablespoons argan or pine nut oil
32 almond blossoms
salt

Method:

Toast the almonds in a dry frying pan, shaking it constantly, for a few seconds. Remove from the heat and set aside.

Melt the butter in a heavy-based saucepan. Add the onions and cook over a low heat, stirring occasionally, until caramelized. Reserve 40 of the almonds for the garnish and add the remainder, with the pine nuts and squash, to the pan. Season with salt and pour in the wine, followed by the stock. Cook for about 10 minutes, until the squash is tender. Add the milk and cream and simmer for 10 minutes. Whisk the mixture with a hand-held blender, strain, then process in a food processor or blender until frothy. Ladle the soup into individual bowls.

Scatter with the reserved almonds, the parsley leaves and almond blossom. Just before serving, drizzle with the argan or pine nut oil.

Chef's tip I agree wholeheartedly with the proverb of our neighbouring village, Cucuronne: 'Cucuronnais, bring in your squash'. I store this winter vegetable in my cellar until spring. Stored in this way, squash continue to develop their flavour and vitamins. I don't discard the seeds either, but wash and dry them to prevent them from going mouldy, then I replant them. Butternut squash works amazingly well in tarts, bacon soufflés and soups. As the name suggests, it has the flavour and shape of a peanut. I highlight this distinctive flavour, which mellows on cooking, by combining it with almonds, pine nuts and argan oil (available from Moroccan delicatessens). Pine nuts enhance the creamy flavour of the butternut squash and add spicier notes of pine resin and almond, while almond blossom counterbalances the creamy flavour which would otherwise be too sweet.

Chicken consommé with egg yolks and wild cherry blossom

Serves 4

Preparation time: 35 minutes
Cooking time: 1 hour 10 minutes

Ingredients:
1 free-range, organic chicken
with giblets
100 g/3½ oz butter
7 tablespoons olive oil
4 garlic cloves, unpeeled and chopped
2 onions, unpeeled and chopped
1 celery stick

1 leek
1 carrot
3 parsnips
250 ml/8 fl oz white wine
1 bay leaf
8 cardamom seeds
1 wild cherry blossom, cultivated cherry
blossom or almond blossom sprig
2 pinches of sugar
7 tablespoons port
7 tablespoons kirsch
4 egg yolks
salt

Method:
Preheat the oven to 240°C (475°F), Gas Mark 9. Place the chicken, with its giblets, in a flameproof casserole. Add the butter and half the oil and roast until golden brown all over. Add the garlic, onions and all the vegetables.

Transfer the casserole to the hob and stir in the wine, scraping any sediment from the base with a wooden spoon. Add 2 litres/3½ pints water, the bay leaf, cardamom, blossom sprig, salt and sugar. Cover and simmer gently for 20 minutes. Be careful not to allow the mixture to boil or it will become cloudy.
Set the chicken aside. Strain the stock and adjust the seasoning, if necessary. (If you like, you can accentuate the golden colour by adding burnt caramel.)

Remove the liver and one of the chicken breasts and dice both.
Dice one of the parsnips.
Divide the diced chicken, liver and parsnip and the cardamom seeds among individual soup bowls. Pour in the port, kirsch and stock.
Garnish with cherry or almond blossom and drizzle with the remaining olive oil, then add a raw egg yolk to each bowl and serve immediately.

Chef's tip The wild cherry tree is known in France as the *merisier des oiseaux*, or 'cherry tree of the birds', because it is so popular with birds. This inspired me to combine it with egg. Egg thickens the consommé and adds some necessary fat, while the sweetness of the parsnip counterbalances the dry fruity flavour of the cherry blossom and the sharp taste of the cardamom. This soup may be enjoyed at any time of day, either at the start or the end of a meal.

Chilled Jerusalem artichoke, borage and rape flower soup

Serves 4

Preparation time: 30 minutes
Cooking time: 45 minutes

Ingredients:

1 kg/2 lb Jerusalem artichokes
2 tablespoons olive oil
1 onion, finely chopped
250 ml/8 fl oz white wine
250 ml/8 fl oz chicken stock (see page 184) or veal stock (see page 185)
250 ml/8 fl oz milk
250 ml/8 fl oz single cream
½ teaspoon sugar
1 litre/1¾ pints groundnut oil
20 vegetable-filled Roman ravioli
1 handful borage flowers
1 handful rape flowers
4 tablespoons truffle oil
salt

Method:

Peel and dice the Jerusalem artichokes immediately before using them. Heat the olive oil in a large saucepan. Add the onion and artichokes and cook until the onion is soft and translucent. Stir in the white wine, gently scraping up any sediment from the base of the pan with a wooden spoon.

Add the stock, milk, cream, sugar and salt and simmer for 25 minutes. When the mixture has reduced, process in a food processor or blender, then pass it through a sieve into a bowl. If the soup is too thick, thin it with a little water or milk. Set aside to cool completely, then chill in the refrigerator.

Heat the groundnut oil in a deep-fryer or large saucepan to 180–190°C/ (350–375°F) or until a cube of bread browns in 30 seconds. Deep-fry the Roman ravioli until golden.

Divide the chilled soup among individual bowls. Garnish with deep-fried ravioli, sprinkle with the flowers and truffle oil and serve immediately. At the restaurant, I serve this soup over a crème brûlée with herb juice.

Chef's tip Jerusalem artichokes are still in the ground in March. Pull them up to create space in your garden. I plant this vegetable at the end of winter for no fewer than five reasons. They have been crucial in the history of poor French farmers since the end of World War II. A single Jerusalem artichoke produces a crop of 25 kg/55 lb. I have been replanting the same Jerusalem artichokes for six years, as they do not degenerate at all. As they can reach a height of 2 metres/6½ feet, it is a good idea to plant them at the edge of your property to form a hedge. They also make excellent fodder for pigs. I make fertilizer by crushing them into the soil and I use the flowers, which resemble little suns, to decorate my hotel. Despite its reputation as a poor man's vegetable, it really is a first-class crop. You just need to use your imagination. I cook it all the time in spring.

Mackerel pie with pigeon livers and 'old boy's jam'

Serves 4

Preparation time: 1 hour
Resting time: 12 hours
Cooking time: 2 hours
Maceration and standing
after cooking: 24 hours
Maceration of grapes: 2 months

Ingredients:
20 mackerel fillets
10 pigeon livers
1 egg
1 garlic clove, chopped
5 g/¼ oz leek, green leaves, finely chopped
5 g/¼ oz spinach, finely chopped
5 g/¼ oz angelica leaves, finely chopped
4 teaspoons Cognac
10 g/⅓ oz cooked spelt
(or cooked wheat grains)

25 g/1 oz pork fat or pork cheek, cubed
5 g/¼ oz capers
4 teaspoons milk
25g/1 oz breadcrumbs
5 g/¼ oz parsley, chopped
50 ml/2 fl oz fish jelly
50 ml/2 fl oz poultry jelly

Pastry:
250 g/8 oz plain flour
50 g/2 oz salt
175 g/6 oz butter
1 small egg
1 small egg yolk
pinch of ground cumin

Old boy's jam:
1 kg/2 lb muscat grapes, not too ripe
3 tablespoons sugar
1 litre/1¾ pints marc brandy

Method:

The jam should be prepared at least two months in advance, unless you have some left from the previous season. Place the grapes in a sterilized jar, sprinkle with the sugar and then pour on the marc brandy. Seal and store.

The day before you are going to cook the pie, prepare the pastry. Place all the ingredients in a bowl and mix together with an electric mixer fitted with dough hooks to make a smooth dough. Leave to rest overnight.

Cut 5 mackerel fillets into cubes (reserve the others). Slice the pigeon livers into 2–3 pieces.

Mix together half the fish cubes and half the livers. Combine with the egg, garlic, leek, spinach, angelica and Cognac. Add the spelt, pork fat, capers, milk, breadcrumbs and chopped parsley. Mix in the remaining mackerel cubes and livers and leave in the refrigerator overnight.

Roll out about two-thirds of the pastry and use to line a mould. Place the whole fish fillets in the pastry case and top with the stuffing. Roll out the remaining pastry, cover the pie, trim the edges and decorate with trimmings (flowers, leaves, etc.). Make a hole in the centre of the lid and insert a pie funnel made of rolled foil. Cook for 2 hours in a preheated oven, 140°C (275°F), Gas Mark 1.

Remove the pie from the mould. Melt both jellies in a small pan over a low heat and pour into the pie through the funnel. Leave to stand for about 12 hours. Serve the pie at room temperature, with the 'old boy's jam'.

Chef's tip You can replace the pastry with caul fat. In this case, cook the pie for 1½ hours at 110°C (225°F), Gas Mark ¼. I always prepare this pie the day before. Instead of selling fizzy drinks, the cafés of Lyon used to display big pots of *confiture de vieux garçon* made of green fruits, especially walnuts traditionally picked around Saint Jean's feast day. These grapes were eaten like gherkins. My grandfather used to make a less refined version without sugar, and enjoyed eating his 'jam' with a sponge finger at the end of a meal.

Little snail stews with a 'tobacco' of Luberon herbs

Serves 4

Preparation time: 40 minutes

Cooking time: 3 hours 45 minutes

Infusion time: 20 minutes

Ingredients:

24 petit-gris snails, starved for 3 days, or canned Burgundy snails

2 litres/3½ pints court-bouillon

50 g/2 oz butter

2 garlic bulbs, chopped

½ bunch coriander, chopped

½ bunch mint, chopped

½ bunch marjoram, chopped

½ bunch flat leaf parsley, chopped

1 fennel bulb, leaves only, chopped

125 ml/4 fl oz white wine

125 ml/4 fl oz semi-skimmed milk

125 ml/4 fl oz crème fraîche

75 g/3 oz chicken stock granules

½ teaspoon granulated sugar

50 ml/2 fl oz white wine vinegar

1 bouquet garni (bay leaf, celery, thyme, rosemary, sage)

salt

Method:

Wash the fresh snails thoroughly, then cook in lightly salted, boiling water for 30 minutes. Drain and refresh under cold water. Remove them from their shells, rinse well in several changes of cold water and cook in the court-bouillon for a further 3 hours.

Heat the butter in a saucepan. When it starts to foam, add the chopped garlic and cook over a low heat, without colouring, until softened. Add all the chopped herbs and cook over a low heat, for 3 minutes, then pour in the white wine and reduce for 3 minutes. Add the milk, the crème fraîche and 125 ml/4 fl oz of the cooking liquid from the snails or the can juices if using canned snails. Stir in the stock granules, sugar, vinegar and bouquet garni and season to taste with salt. Bring to the boil, cover, then remove from the heat and leave to infuse for 20 minutes.

Remove and discard the bouquet garni. Process the sauce in a food processor or blender, strain and adjust the seasoning. Keep warm.

Drain the snails, arrange them in small dishes and coat generously with the frothy sauce. Serve hot.

Chef's tip Wild tobacco, which used to be called *petit-chêne* – 'little oak' – can be gathered in spring and early autumn in the hollows and valleys of Luberon. As an infusion, it is said to purify the body and the blood. I often add it to other dried chopped herbs and call this mixture a tobacco of Luberon herbs.

Court-bouillon of baby turnips with seasonal truffles

Serves 4

Preparation time: 40 minutes

Cooking time: 40 minutes

Ingredients:

750 ml/1¼ pints chicken
stock (see page 184)

3 pinches of sugar

3 tablespoons port

32 baby turnips, peeled with
green tops intact

4 truffles

3 tablespoons truffle oil

3 tablespoons olive oil

salt

Method:

Pour the stock into a large saucepan. Add the sugar and port and heat gently until the stock starts to simmer.

Add the baby turnips and cook gently for 15 minutes, then remove from the pan with a slotted spoon. Strain the stock through a coffee filter or muslin-lined sieve. Season to taste with salt.

Brush the truffles under cold running water, slice thinly and divide among individual soup bowls.

Add the turnips and pour in the strained court-bouillon, then flavour with truffle oil and olive oil.

Serve immediately while still hot.

Chef's tip This spring consommé celebrates the soil by including turnips and truffles. Port enhances the flavour of the truffles, while sugar balances the slight bitterness of the turnips. You can prepare a chicken stock using just fillets, rather than the carcass, which can then be chopped into cubes and used to garnish the court-bouillon.

The flowering
of the very first wild plants

Early shoots in the Luberon.
Above: Budding lilac.
Above right: Violet.
Opposite above: Wild
thyme blossom.
Opposite below: The white
blossom of the cherry and
almond trees that will
adorn the plates and tables
of the Moulin.

In mid-March nature begins – slowly – to emerge from its winter slumber. Tender wild asparagus spears are scattered along the paths and by the rivers – the locals combine them with other vegetables, while Édouard prefers to use them as a garnish. Among the rocks the earliest succulents are now visible, but the juniper berries on the way to Couturas and on the hillside are still black and bitter. The riverbank is a carpet of wild watercress shoots; chives, garlic and wild leeks nestle in the valleys and among the bushes. Sorrel buds are dotted along the fields and the river's edge. Rocket flowers where the soil is lighter beside the lanes and in the vineyards, while the cruciferous plants, such as mustard and rape, offer a colourful splash of golden-yellow. The violet announces the arrival of Easter – it is Édouard's favourite in a salad, as an infusion or even as a liqueur. This seasonal timetable inspires his recipes. Remembering that angelica flowers early, he shouts out to his *pâtissier*, 'David, have a think about an Easter pre-dessert based on an angelica ice cream with egg mimosa. And also a rich sauce over the ice cream, with a slight woody aroma and a touch of *amarena*, would you?'

After the violet comes the orchid. Were it not that it has been a protected species since the 1960s, he would happily offer it in a sabayon with a grapefruit gratin. Still, he has wild red carnations and wild roses for infusions, jonquil (as an ice cream served with a cassis flavoured, dark chocolate beignet) and many more...

Hybrid salsify flowers

Eggs, tarts and pies

Eggs in nests, with a delicate infusion of catmint and chive flower fritters •
Tart with a wild herb and chicken titbit filling • Artichoke, red chard and veal
kidney pie • Fried eggs studded with juniper berries from 'la Grande Ourse'
and Monalisa potatoes from Pertius cooked in embers • Spiral shallot tart with
woodland aromas • Bouillabaisse of eggs with wild cress and St George's
mushrooms • Parcels of baby leeks, with milk and smoked quail's eggs •
Courgettes filled with tomato and basil sorbet, served with olive oil • Chilled
'agastache' soup and chanterelle mousseline with truffle oil

Eggs in nests, with a delicate infusion of catmint and chive flower fritters

Serves 8

Preparation time: 40 minutes

Cooking time: 20 minutes

Ingredients:

1 large bunch of catmint
(or another wild herb)

4 tablespoons chicken stock
(see page 184)

250 ml/8 fl oz white wine

7 tablespoons milk

150 ml/¼ pint crème fraîche

4 tablespoons plain flour

15 g/½ oz cornflour

drop of white wine vinegar

24 quail's eggs

1 litre/1¾ pints oil, for deep frying

24 chive flowers

salt and pepper

Method:

Place 2 of the catmint sprigs in a bowl. Bring the stock and 4 tablespoons of the wine to the boil, then pour into the bowl, cover and leave to infuse for 5 minutes. Reserve 4 small catmint sprigs for garnish. Strain the infusion into a clean pan and blend with the remaining catmint, the milk and crème fraîche. Season with salt and pepper. Cook over a low heat for 10 minutes.

Make the batter for the fritters by whisking together the flour, cornflour, a pinch of salt and the remaining white wine until smooth.

Fill a high-sided frying pan with water, bring to simmering point and add the vinegar. Break the eggs into a cup, 1 at a time, add to the pan and poach them, in 2–3 batches, in the simmering water for barely 1 minute. Lift them out with a slotted spoon and immerse immediately in iced water to prevent any further cooking. Drain on a clean tea towel.

Heat the oil in a deep-fryer or large saucepan to 180–190°C/350–375°F or until a cube of bread browns in 30 seconds. Dip the chive flowers into the batter to coat, then cook in the hot oil until crisp and golden. Drain on a tea towel or kitchen paper before seasoning with salt.

To serve, spoon the hot sauce on to warmed plates. Arrange the fritters and eggs alternately on the plates, and garnish each plate with the reserved catmint sprigs.

The eggs and chive flower fritters should be eaten together.

Chef's tip Catmint grows in little tufts resembling mint. They give off a strong smell which attracts cats, hence the herb's name. The taste is very earthy and reminiscent of beef and blood, with a hint of menthol.

Tart with a wild herb and chicken titbit filling

Serves 4

Preparation time: 45 minutes
Chilling time: 20 minutes
Cooking time: 25 minutes

Ingredients:

1 quantity puff pastry
(see page 187)
1 handful spinach, about 90 g/3¼ oz
1 leek, green leaves only, about 50 g/2 oz
1 handful lettuce, about 50 g/2 oz
1 handful sorrel, about 50 g/2 oz
2 ribs of Swiss chard with leaves

2 eggs, lightly beaten
50 ml/2 fl oz crème fraîche
25 g/1 oz mature goat's cheese or mature
Gruyère or Parmesan cheese, grated
2 tablespoons finely chopped tarragon
2 tablespoons finely chopped parsley
2 tablespoons finely chopped savory
grated nutmeg, to taste
20 g/¾ oz butter
giblets of 4 chickens, such as livers, hearts,
parson's nose (ask your butcher to order
them), finely diced
3 tablespoons veal stock (see page 185)
2 angelica leaves
salt and pepper

Method:

Prepare the pastry according to the instructions on page 189. Leave to rest for 30 minutes.

Blanch the spinach, leek, lettuce, sorrel and Swiss chard briefly in boiling water, drain and refresh under cold water, then drain again and chop coarsely with a knife. Mix with the beaten eggs, half the crème fraîche, the cheese, chopped herbs and nutmeg, pepper and salt to taste.

Melt the butter in a frying pan. Add the diced giblets and cook for 30 seconds in the hot butter.

Roll out the pastry on a lightly floured surface and use to line a small tart tin. Chill for 20 minutes.

Fill the pastry case, first with a layer of giblets and then with a layer of the herb mixture. Cook the pie in a preheated oven, 220°C (425°F), Gas Mark 7, for 10 minutes. Add the remaining crème fraîche, return the pie to the oven and bake for a further 10 minutes. Remove from the oven and leave to cool.

Bring the veal stock to a simmer in a small pan with the angelica and cook for 1 minute. Just before serving, spoon the hot stock over the top of the tart.

Chef's tip Corsican cheese has a strong salty flavour and can be used to counterbalance the sweetness of the wild herbs. This recipe is similar to a quiche, but the surface is glazed with the savory flavoured veal stock in the same way as gravy is poured over meat.

Artichoke, red chard and veal kidney pie

Serves 4

Preparation time: 45 minutes

Cooking time: 25 minutes

Ingredients:

250 g/8 oz bread dough
(see page 146)

4 globe artichoke hearts

100 ml/3½ fl oz white wine

3 ribs of red chard with leaves

50 ml/2 fl oz veal stock (see page 185)

1 egg

100 g/3½ oz peas and broad beans, shelled

1 bunch of radishes, thinly sliced

50 ml/2 fl oz vinaigrette (see page 184)

½ veal kidney, cored and diced

8 small fresh anchovy or sardine fillets

salt and pepper

parsley leaves, to garnish

Method:

Roll out the dough on a lightly floured surface and use to line a tart tin. Cook in a preheated oven, 250°C (480°F), Gas Mark 10, for 5 minutes. Reduce the oven temperature to 200°C (400°F), Gas Mark 6 and cook for a further 5 minutes. Remove from the oven and set aside.

Cook the artichoke hearts in a pan of water mixed with the white wine for 10 minutes. Drain and cut into quarters.

Separate the chard ribs from the leaves. Cut the ribs into batons.

Boil the ribs for 6 minutes and the leaves for 3 minutes. Drain. Mix the chard leaves with the veal stock and then mix in the egg. Season with salt and pepper.

Mix together the radishes and the peas and broad beans in a serving bowl, then toss with the vinaigrette.

Pour the mixture of chard leaves, stock and egg into the base of the pastry case. Cover with the artichoke hearts, chard rib batons and diced kidney and top with the fish fillets. Cook in a preheated oven, 220°C (425°F), Gas Mark 7, for 6–8 minutes. Serve hot, garnished with parsley leaves and accompanied by the spring salad of raw vegetables.

Chef's tip This dish uses the recipe for bread dough with cedar, spruce and cypress pine nuts, but omits the pine nuts. The kidney gives a chewy firmness to the soft buttery texture of the chard, which is known as *bettes à cochon*, 'pig's chard'. The sour flavour of the peas and broad beans contrasts sharply with the chard and moist bread. This fresh-tasting dish is perfect for enjoying in the sun.

Fried eggs studded with juniper berries from 'la Grande Ourse' and Monalisa potatoes from Pertius cooked in embers

Serves 4

Preparation time: 15 minutes

Cooking time: 35 minutes

Ingredients:

4 Monalisa or other red-skinned potatoes

8 small juniper branches

1 tablespoon olive oil

75 g/3 oz butter

8 juniper berries, chopped

8 free-range eggs

salt and pepper

Method:

Rinse the potatoes without peeling them and wrap individually in squares of foil.

Prepare some embers by setting light to the juniper sprigs in a pan and placing the pan at the bottom of the oven. Add the potatoes and cook in the embers for 30 minutes.

Heat the oil and 50 g/2 oz of the butter in a frying pan, preferably one made of copper. Add the juniper berries, salt and pepper. Break the eggs into the frying pan and fry for just 1 minute.

Cut the potatoes in half, top with a knob of butter, add an egg to each half and serve immediately.

Chef's tip Copper is an excellent conductor of heat. If you use a copper frying pan, you will barely need to return the eggs to the hob. This recipe will produce smooth whites. It is important to sprinkle salt on the fat and not directly on the egg, to avoid spots on the yolk. La Grande Ourse is the name of the Emmanuels' land where Édouard's team gathers juniper berries.

Spiral shallot tart with woodland aromas

Serves 4

Preparation time: 45 minutes

Cooking time: 35 minutes

Ingredients:

32 Simiane or other large shallots, peeled

250 g/8 oz flaky pastry,

rolled out

2 tablespoons sugar

125 g/4 oz butter

4 tablespoons clear honey

10 juniper berries

125 g/4 oz wild salad vegetables

or mixed green salad

2 tablespoons vinaigrette (see page 184)

salt and pepper

Method:

Blanch the whole shallots in boiling water for 5 minutes, drain and set aside. Line a tart dish with the flaky pastry, prick the base with a fork and dust with the sugar.

Melt the butter in a large, heavy-based frying pan. Add the shallots and fry until lightly golden and caramelized, adding the honey and juniper berries. Season with salt and pepper.

Using a spoon, remove the shallots from the pan, one by one, and carefully arrange them in a spiral in the base of the pastry case.

Cook in a preheated oven, 220°C (425°F), Gas Mark 7, for 15–20 minutes. Serve this tart warm, garnished with a salad dressed with vinaigrette.

Chef's tip This tart will always remind me of buffets, picnics, a sandwich in the smokehouse...Thanks to the presence of juniper berries, it smells of woodland and musky damp soil. Simiane shallots and onions are a Provençal variety characterized by their pink colour and large bulbs. They are delightful fried in butter. Serving them in a tart accentuates their sweetness, and gives them a slight braised flavour which brings out their juices.

Bouillabaisse of eggs with wild cress and St George's mushrooms

Serves 4

Preparation time: 30 minutes
Cooking time: 25 minutes

Ingredients:
4 nettle leaves
1 bunch of wild cress or
garden cress
250 ml/8 fl oz chicken stock
(see page 184), boiling

5 potatoes, peeled and diced
12 St George's mushrooms or oyster
mushrooms, coarsely chopped
2 garlic cloves, peeled
½ teaspoon tomato purée
1 egg yolk
150 ml/¼ pint olive oil
1 drop of white wine vinegar
4 eggs
4 slices of bread
salt and pepper

Method:

Remove the stalks from the nettles and cress and rinse the leaves. Set the nettles aside. Place the cress leaves in a bowl, pour over the boiling stock, cover and set aside to infuse for 5 minutes before straining. Reserve the chicken stock.

Bring the stock back to simmering point, then add the potatoes and cook for 15 minutes. Remove from the pan with a slotted spoon.

Poach the mushrooms in the stock for 1 minute, then remove with a slotted spoon. Poach the nettle leaves in the stock for 2 minutes.

Prepare the rouille. Take the equivalent of 1 potato – one-fifth of the cooked potato cubes – and mash with the garlic. Stir in the tomato purée, egg yolk, 125 ml/4 fl oz of the oil, salt and pepper. Bring some water to simmering point in a large saucepan and add the vinegar. Break the 4 eggs individually and poach them in the water for 3 minutes, until the white is just firm. Remove with a slotted spoon and drain on a clean tea towel.

Toast the bread on both sides. Divide the vegetables among 4 soup plates. Pour on the hot stock, and add a poached egg and a drop of oil. Serve with the rouille and the toasted bread.

Chef's tip This dish is a variant of pistou soup, with rouille instead of the pistou. You can serve it straight out of the pan. Wild cress has a sharp taste similar to raw nettles and cucumber. Garden cress can be used instead of wild cress. Cooked nettle leaves have a metallic flavour tinged with iodine and a firm texture, unlike other leafy vegetables. St. George's mushrooms are gathered at the end of spring and taste good when they are barely cooked and still firm.

Parcels of baby leeks,
with milk and smoked quail's eggs

Serves 4	**Ingredients:**
	16 baby leeks, trimmed
Preparation time: 40 minutes	1 teaspoon white wine vinegar
Cooking: time 35 minutes	24 quail's eggs
Smoking time: 30 minutes	1 juniper branch
	250 g/8 oz bread dough
	(see page 146)
	52 juniper berries
	500 ml/17 fl oz milk
	2 tablespoons cornflour
	salt and pepper
	8 parsley sprigs, to garnish
	Parmesan shavings, to serve

Method:

Cook the leeks in salted, boiling water for 15 minutes, then drain.

Reserve the cooking liquid. It can be chilled and served as a drink to accompany this dish.

Bring a pan of water to simmering point and add the vinegar. Break the quail's eggs and poach for 1 minute, then remove from the pan with a slotted spoon. Drain on a clean tea towel and spread out on a plate. Put the plate on the top shelf of the oven; do not switch the oven on. Set light to the juniper branch and place it on a roasting tin underneath. Leave the eggs to absorb the fragrant smoke for 30 minutes. Grease 4 individual pie dishes with butter, line them with bread dough and then stand the leeks upright inside the dough (cut them in half if they are too long). If you like, you can fold over the edges of the dough to form a purse shape. Cook in a preheated oven, 225°C (425°F), Gas Mark 7, for 20 minutes, then remove from the oven and turn out.

Cut 20 juniper berries in half, drop them into the milk in a pan and simmer for 5 minutes. Stir the cornflour to a paste with a little water, then stir into the milk and bring to the boil, stirring constantly. Pour the milk mixture into serving dishes, add a parcel of leeks and surround with the eggs. Garnish with the remaining juniper berries and the parsley before serving with freshly ground pepper and Parmesan shavings.

Chef's tip The white and green leaves of the leek are beautifully crunchy when cooked. I adore the contrast between cold eggs and warm milk. This dish cries out for freshly ground pepper and Parmesan cheese (sprinkle with Parmesan shavings before serving). You can garnish this dish by mixing 2 raw egg yolks with a drop of oil and salt and using this mixture to draw artistic flourishes in the juniper milk.

*In the tradition of yesteryear, Édouard intersperses his courses with delicacies which
refresh the palate and sharpen the appetite, such as fresh sorbets and vinegary consommés. A time to pause and savour.*

Courgettes filled with tomato and basil sorbet, served with olive oil

Serves 4

Preparation time: 30 minutes
Cooking time: 20 minutes
Freezing time: 45 minutes

Ingredients:

4 small round courgettes

500 g/1 lb ripe, deep red tomatoes

1 bunch of basil

100 ml/3½ fl oz olive oil, plus extra
for sprinkling

5 celery leaves

1 tablespoon sugar

1½ tablespoons salt

½ teaspoon pepper

4 tablespoons lemon juice

coarse salt

Method:

Cut the tops off the courgettes, leaving the stem. Make sure that the bases are level so that they stand upright, then scoop out the flesh using a spoon. Cook the bases in salted, boiling water for 15 minutes and the tops for 10 minutes.

Place the tomatoes in a food processor. Reserve 4 basil sprigs for the garnish and add the remainder to the food processor with the olive oil, celery, sugar, salt and pepper. Process to a purée, push through a sieve and freeze in a sorbet maker.

Sprinkle the courgette shells with salt and lemon juice. Pour in a drop of olive oil and place the courgettes in the refrigerator so that the olive oil congeals. To serve, fill the courgette shells with a ball of sorbet and replace the tops. Garnish each plate with a sprig of basil, a few grains of coarse salt and a drop of oil. Serve immediately.

Chef's tip In our garden, we pick courgettes morning and night in the quest for the perfect courgette, which should be neither too big nor too little. At the market, you can find small round courgettes which are perfect for this recipe. If you don't own a sorbet maker, you can always make a granita by placing a dish of the mixture in the freezer for 3–4 hours, and stirring with a fork as soon as the ice crystals begin to form, about every 30 minutes.

Chilled 'agastache' soup and chanterelle mousseline with truffle oil

Serves 4

Preparation time: 30 minutes
Cooking time: 25 minutes

Ingredients:
500 g/1 lb courgettes
½ bunch of mint
4 star anise
1½ tablespoons chicken stock powder
500 ml/17 fl oz chicken stock
(see page 184), boiling

50 g/2 oz sugar
150 ml/¼ pint white wine vinegar
100 g/3½ oz butter
500 g/1 lb grey chanterelle mushrooms, peeled and chopped
100 ml/3½ fl oz ruby port
100 ml/3½ fl oz Cognac
100 ml/3½ fl oz single cream
50 ml/2 fl oz double cream, whipped
a few drops of truffle oil
4 thin slices of fresh truffle
salt

Method:

Steam the courgettes for 15 minutes. Once cooled, drain and place in a blender. Reserve 4 mint sprigs for the garnish and put the remaining leaves in the blender, with the star anise and chicken stock powder.

Process the mixture, gradually adding the boiling stock. Strain and chill.

Add salt and sugar to taste, and vinegar to adjust the acidity and freshness of this soup. Melt the butter in a pan and cook the mushrooms until they have yielded up all their liquid. Stir in the port and Cognac, scraping up any sediment from the base of the pan, then cook for 3 minutes to reduce.

Pour in the single cream and cook gently for a further 10 minutes over a medium heat, until thickened. Process in a blender and push through a sieve. Leave to cool, then gently fold in the whipped double cream.

Arrange a dome of the mushroom mousseline in the centre of 4 soup bowls. Pour the chilled soup around the mousseline, drizzle with truffle oil, garnish with a slice of truffle and a sprig of mint and serve immediately.

Chef's tip If you like, just use the trimmings of the mushrooms for this mousseline and keep the caps for frying. The spiciness of the mousseline contrasts with the sweet nutty flavour of the courgettes. Agastache is a plant which tastes of mint and aniseed, and this recipe uses mint and star anise in its place. This dish may also be served as a starter.

Pruning trees and vines

Newly pruned,
the vines and fruit trees will soon
be heavy with lush, succulent fruit.

During his walks, armed with his secateurs, Édouard cuts back the branches of the almond and cherry trees, which he will use in his liqueurs or to garnish his dishes.

The first pruning of the almond and apricot trees is at the beginning of March. As the trees bear fruit only every two years, the youngest shoots are re-trimmed at the end of the month to prevent them needlessly drawing on the sap. In pruning fruit trees, preserving the sap is paramount; the same goes for grape vines. In May, at Constantin Chevalier, one of Édouard's wine suppliers, they sacrifice the lowest branches and, depending on how much wine they wish to produce, they retain only one or two . Each branch then grows two to three offshoots with maybe five or six bunches of grapes. Any branch in the shade also has to go – the grapes must soak up as much sun as possible. The cuttings will serve to flavour grilled and smoked ingredients. In June it will be time to lift the branches back on to the wires, then to get rid of the weeds – but not wild rocket, which does no harm. During July the vines will be thinned to stop them becoming tangled and overgrown. They must stand straight and have maximum sunlight and air, both for their health and to help pollination. Next, it is time to trim the excess leaves. If there are too many grapes, there will be a *vendange verte* (a harvest of the green grapes). Édouard has been known to use these unripe grapes in a *confiture de vieux garçon* (old boy's jam).

Pruning the olive trees does not follow the same pattern as for fruit trees. It takes place during November and December, as to do it between March and May would be risky with the return of the frosts still possible. In spring, they have to make do with a trim.

It is this judicious care and pruning which affords Provence its landscape: the twisted branches of the vine, the silver-grey of the olive tree and the white blossom of the almond.

Little by little
the fruit fills out and grows
heavy on the branch.

Fish and seafood

Breton lobster braised in Lourmarin almond milk • Sea urchins in their shells, with sea urchin butter • Mignonnette of conger eel and red gurnard with vervain and a vegetable garnish • Monkfish with chamomile and lovage, garnished with broad beans, wild poppies and angelica-flavoured gazpacho • Sea squirts in a germander marinade, saltwort salad with nigella flowers and chilled purslane gazpacho • Salad of wakame with borage flowers and Lourmarin olive oil • Fried frogs' legs with wormwood and wild garlic sauce • Scallops and tempura of young chicory seasoned with lemon balm and broom • Plum blossom in a basket and gratin of langoustines with sabayon sauce • Langoustines with confit of petit-gris snails and peas, coriander jus and young broad beans • Risotto of spelt and clams with spices from the town of Apt • Skate wings poached in a vegetable stock, served over young leaves of New Zealand spinach in a sweet vinaigrette, seasoned with a coulis of oysters with lemon balm • Fillet of exceptional grilled dentex, seasoned with candied orange and cade berries • Turbot braised in whey flavoured with vervain, and early rose potatoes crushed with lemon

Breton lobster braised in
Lourmarin almond milk

Serves 4

Preparation time: 40 minutes

Cooking time: 15 minutes

Ingredients:

1 carrot, thinly sliced

2 onions, thinly sliced

4 bay leaves

1 bunch of flat leaf parsley

2–4 live lobsters

200 g/7 oz toasted almonds

250 ml/8 fl oz almond milk
(see chef's tip, below)

250 ml/8 fl oz single cream

100 ml/3½ fl oz dry white wine

sugar, to taste

16 fresh almonds, plus extra to garnish

200 ml/7 fl oz vinaigrette (see page 184)

16 cherry tomatoes

4 pretty almond tree sprigs

16 salad burnet sprigs

8 strips of orange rind

4 celery leaves

coarsely ground salt

Method:

Put the carrot, onions, bay leaves, flat leaf parsley and some coarsely ground salt in a large pan. Cover generously with cold water, bring to the boil and boil for a few minutes to make a court-bouillon. Immerse the lobsters, bring the liquid back to the boil and cook for 4 minutes at a rapid boil.

Lift out the lobsters with a slotted spoon and leave until cool enough to handle. Reserve and strain 250 ml/8 fl oz of the cooking stock. Bring to the boil, add the toasted almonds and infuse for 10 minutes. Add the almond milk, cream and white wine and cook for a few minutes, then strain, adjust the seasoning, add sugar to taste and the fresh almonds and set aside to infuse.

When the lobsters have cooled, remove and discard their shells. Dip them in the vinaigrette and then sear rapidly under a preheated grill, brushing frequently with the vinaigrette.

Spoon the almond milk on to 4 serving plates and arrange the lobsters and cherry tomatoes on top. Garnish each plate with an almond tree sprig, 2–3 unblanched almonds and 2 sprigs of salad burnet. Add 2 strips of orange rind and 1 teaspoon of vinaigrette.

Chef's tip Almond trees are a popular crop in Lourmarin. Having these pretty trees on my doorstep has inspired me to include almonds in my recipes, especially in spring when they are white and tender. I love to use sweet fresh almonds to garnish my dishes and to make almond milk. I blend fresh blanched almonds with milk and leave to soak for three or four days in the refrigerator. I then use this milk to prepare sauces which are perfect with shellfish, such as this lobster, shellfish sauces and stocks.

Sea urchins in their shells, with sea urchin butter

Serves 4

Preparation time: 1 hour
Cooking time: 50 minutes

Ingredients:
50 ml/2 fl oz olive oil
22 sea urchins
50 ml/2 fl oz Cognac

1 thyme sprig, chopped
1 bay leaf
½ onion, chopped
1 carrot, chopped
5 garlic cloves, crushed
5 coriander seeds, crushed
100 ml/3½ fl oz white wine
1 teaspoon tomato purée
½ teaspoon sugar
200 ml/7 fl oz milk
500 ml/17 fl oz crème fraîche
50 g/2 oz butter, diced
2 large egg whites
350 g/11½ oz conger eel, boned
2 shallots
salt and pepper

Method:

Heat 2 tablespoons of the oil in a flameproof casserole. Add 10 sea urchins and brown them all over, then crush them in the casserole using the base of a bottle or a pestle. Add the Cognac and ignite. When the flames have died down, add the thyme, bay leaf, onion, carrot, garlic and coriander. Add the white wine and bring to the boil, scraping up any sediment from the base of the casserole with a wooden spoon to deglaze.

Stir in the tomato purée and sugar and season with salt and pepper to taste. Pour 150 ml/¼ pint of the milk, 150 ml/¼ pint of the crème fraîche and 300 ml/½ pint water into the casserole, then simmer gently until reduced by half. Process with a hand-held blender and strain. Gradually mix in the butter and blend again.

Whisk the egg whites until stiff. Process the conger eel with the shallots, then press through a sieve. Stir in the remaining crème fraîche and milk and 50 ml/2 fl oz of the cooled sea urchin bisque. Season with salt and pepper. Gently fold in the whisked egg whites.

Open the remaining sea urchins using kitchen scissors. Carefully remove their corals and reserve. Fill the sea urchin shells with a ball of stuffing moulded with an ice cream scoop.

Braise for 3 minutes. Decorate the shells with strips of coral arranged in a star shape, place on a flameproof dish and brown for 5 minutes under a preheated grill. Pour the sauce on to plates and divide the sea urchins among them.

Chef's tip The fish stuffing will become light and fluffy under the heat of the grill, like quenelles. These quantities will allow you to stuff up to 5 sea urchins per person. It is difficult to prepare this stuffing in smaller amounts. If you feel like it, increase the number of sea urchins. Sea urchins go well with Cognac. Their flavours of iodine and peat, evocative of the ocean and spices, complement one another superbly. Feel free to adjust the seasoning with a splash of Cognac.

Mignonnette of conger eel and red gurnard with vervain and a vegetable garnish

Serves 4	250 ml/8 fl oz milk
	250 ml/8 fl oz single cream
Preparation time: 1 hour	2 lemons, peeled and diced
Cooking time: 35 minutes	1 bay leaf
	½ teaspoon sugar
Ingredients:	260 g/8 oz plus 1½ tablespoons plain flour
1.5 kg/3 lb conger eel	2 Charlotte or other waxy potatoes, halved
4 red gurnards, each 400 g/13 oz	4 carrots, peeled with leaf tops intact
50 ml/2 fl oz olive oil	1 leek, cut into 1 cm/½ inch slices
2 shallots, finely chopped	25 g/1 oz shelled petits pois
1 large bunch of vervain	12 cherry tomatoes
500 ml/17 fl oz white wine	1 egg, lightly beaten with
	1 tablespoon water
	2 teaspoons coarse salt
	fine salt

Method:

Cut the conger eel into 1.5 cm/¾ inch chunks. Remove the central bone, then cut the flesh into 20 cubes, about 1 cm/½ inch. Fillet the red gurnards. If they are small (5 cm/2 inches in length), leave them whole, otherwise slice them.

Heat half the oil in a large pan, add the conger eel and the shallots and cook until lightly browned.

Chop 5 of the vervain sprigs. Pour the white wine, milk and cream into the pan and add the lemon, chopped vervain, bay leaf, sugar and salt. Simmer gently for 15 minutes.

Place 4 remaining vervain sprigs in a heatproof bowl and strain the wine and milk mixture over them. Keep warm over a pan of barely simmering water.

In another bowl, mix the flour with 100 ml/3½ fl oz water to form a paste.

Cook the potatoes, carrots, leek and petits pois in a pan of boiling water for 10–15 minutes, adding the tomatoes about 5 minutes before the end of cooking. Drain well.

Heat the remaining oil and fry the red gurnards on one side. Transfer them to a large casserole or 4 individual casseroles and add the vegetables.

Process the sauce with a hand-held blender until smooth, then half-fill the casserole or casseroles with it.

Cover with the lid or lids and seal with the flour paste. Glaze with the beaten egg mixture and stud with the coarse salt grains. Cook in a preheated oven, 240°C (475°F), Gas Mark 9, for 8–10 minutes if you are using a large casserole, or for 5 minutes for individual casseroles.

Serve the casserole or casseroles on a bed of vervain, and break the crust in front of your guests. The crust should be eaten like a gratin topping with the vegetables.

Chef's tip Conger eel is full of gelatine and the trimmings can be used to make fish soup. Bouillabaisse would not be the same without conger eel. The aroma of vervain quickly evaporates on heating, which is why this sauce should never be boiled once prepared, but should be kept warm in a bain-marie.

Monkfish with chamomile and lovage, garnished with broad beans, wild poppies and angelica-flavoured gazpacho

Serves 4

Preparation time: 1 hour
Cooking time: 40 minutes

Ingredients:

4 monkfish tails, each 300 g/10 oz,
150 ml/¼ pint olive oil
250 ml/8 fl oz white wine
350 ml/12 fl oz fish stock (see page 185)
½ teaspoon jasmine tea
250 ml/8 fl oz milk
100 ml/3½ fl oz single cream
2 tablespoons cornflour
3 wild poppy roots, stems and flowers

1 bunch of vervain
1 small bunch of chamomile (large flowers)
5 lovage sprigs
1 handful of geranium leaves
500 g/1 lb broad beans, shelled
20 g/¾ oz butter
200 g/7 oz Swiss chard
3 tablespoons white wine vinegar
5 g/¼ oz angelica leaves
5 g/¼ oz lovage leaves
3 tablespoons breadcrumbs
3 pinches of sugar
salt and pepper
8 wild poppy flowers and chamomile flowers, to garnish

Method:

Cut off the thin ends of the monkfish tails. Skin the tails and remove the transparent membranes, then set aside. Heat 1 tablespoon of the oil in a pan and brown the fish trimmings. Pour in the white wine and 250 ml/8 fl oz of the stock and simmer for 20 minutes. Strain into a clean pan.

Add the tea, milk and cream, bring to the boil and simmer for 5 minutes.

Mix the cornflour with 1 tablespoon water, stir into the pan and bring back to the boil. Place the wild poppy roots, vervain, chamomile, lovage sprigs and geranium leaves in a bowl and strain the sauce over them. Strain the sauce and process with a hand-held blender.

If the broad beans are very fresh, leave the skins on. If not, blanch the beans in boiling water, drain and pinch between your fingers to remove the skins

Melt the butter with 1 tablespoon of the remaining oil in a large pan and cook the beans for 2 minute. Pour in just enough of the remaining stock to cover the beans and cook for a further 5 minutes.

To make the gazpacho, cook the Swiss chard in boiling water until tender, then drain. Process with 5 tablespoons of the remaining olive oil, 3 ice cubes, the vinegar, angelica and lovage leaves, breadcrumbs, sugar, salt and pepper. Strain and chill in the refrigerator.

Heat the remaining oil in a large ovenproof pan and cook the monkfish over a high heat until just coloured. Transfer to a preheated oven, 240°C (475°F), Gas Mark 9, and cook for 5 minutes.

Spoon a swirl of gazpacho on 4 plates. Sprinkle with the broad beans and add the fish. Pour the sauce into the space in the middle, garnish the edge of the plates with flowers and serve.

Chef's tip I find monkfish similar to meat, especially fillet steak. It has the same texture and is prepared in the same way, for example roasted or in blanquettes. Its dorsal spine looks more like a meat bone than a fish bone. Broad beans should always be served with savory, which is is well known for its aphrodisiac properties.

Sea squirts in a germander marinade, saltwort salad with nigella flowers and chilled purslane gazpacho

Serves 4

Preparation time: 25 minutes

Cooking time: 5 minutes

Ingredients:

16 sea squirts

50 ml/2 fl oz vinaigrette (see page 184)

pinch of ground cumin

10 germander leaves

12 baby octopuses, cleaned

100 g/3½ oz saltwort

24 purslane leaves

Gazpacho:

100 g/3½ oz purslane and spinach, stalks removed

40 ml/1½ fl oz olive oil

1 teaspoon white wine vinegar

2–4 tablespoons fresh lemon juice

a few nigella leaves and seeds (optional)

salt and pepper

Method:

Cut the sea squirts in half, remove from their 'tunics' and soak in the vinaigrette. Mix the cumin and germander leaves into the vinaigrette.

Dry-fry the baby octopuses for a few minutes, until they are firm and crunchy. Keep warm.

To make the gazpacho, briefly blanch the purslane and spinach in boiling water, then drain and refresh under cold water.

Process with the oil, vinegar, lemon juice to taste, 3 ice cubes, salt and pepper in a food processor. Add the nigella leaves and seeds, if using.

Drain the sea squirts, reserving the vinaigrette. Rinse the saltwort and toss with the vinaigrette. Arrange in 4 soup plates, add the purslane leaves, hot baby octopuses and marinated sea squirts, then pour the gazpacho into the dish and serve immediately.

Chef's tip I usually grill baby octopuses, which suits their firm texture. However, you get the same result by dry-frying them in a very hot pan. Sea squirts look like large purplish-blue figs, hence their French nickname *figues de mer*, 'figs of the sea'. They cling to the seaweed along the shores of the Mediterranean and are eaten raw, like sea urchins. You can use rock samphire or New Zealand spinach in place of saltwort. Otherwise, just serve with purslane.

Salad of wakame with borage flowers and Lourmarin olive oil

Serves 4

Preparation time: 10 minutes

Cooking time: 5 minutes

Ingredients:

75 g/3 oz dried wakame seaweed

12 borage flowers with stems

50 ml/2 fl oz olive oil

4 teaspoons white wine vinegar

3 pinches of sugar

24 saltwort sprigs

salt and pepper

Method:

Place the wakame in cold water to rehydrate. Drain when it is tender.

Remove the stems from the borage flowers, reserving stems and flowers. Blanch the borage stems in boiling water, then drain. Blend with the oil, vinegar, 2 ice cubes, sugar, salt and pepper, and then strain.

Divide the saltwort and wakame among 4 dishes. Season with the vinaigrette, sprinkle with the borage flowers and chill before serving.

Chef's tip This fresh crunchy salad is eaten as an appetizer and refreshes the palate. The borage stems give body to the vinaigrette and their oily texture imparts a smoothness to the salad. They also add a slight taste of iodine, like raw cucumber. I consider wakame to be the parsley of the sea. It is available in organic food stores and Asian supermarkets. You can use agar-agar or nori seaweed in place of wakame. (Nori should be blanched for 30 seconds before use.)

Fried frogs' legs with wormwood and wild garlic sauce

Serves 4

Preparation time: 45 minutes
Cooking time: 35 minutes

Ingredients:

24 frogs
100 ml/3½ fl oz olive oil
3 shallots, finely chopped
200 ml/7 fl oz white wine
200 ml/7 fl oz fish stock (see page 185)

200 ml/7 fl oz milk
200 ml/7 fl oz single cream
7 wormwood sprigs
3 tablespoons Chartreuse
1 garlic bulb, peeled
16 potatoes, chopped
100 ml/3½ fl oz thick crème fraîche
100 g/3½ oz soft white cheese
50 g/2 oz plain flour
40 g/1½ oz butter
4 tablespoons fresh lemon juice
1 handful of chive flowers
salt and pepper

Ramsons, sometimes called wild garlic, opens its buds

Method:

Remove the frogs' legs.

Heat 2 tablespoons of the olive oil in a pan and brown the frogs' chests with the shallots. Pour in the wine and simmer for 20 minutes. Add the stock, milk and cream. Simmer for 5 minutes. Season with salt and pepper, then process with a hand-held blender. Put 5 wormwood sprigs in a bowl, strain the sauce over them, add the Chartreuse and reserve.

Reserve 2 garlic cloves and place the remainder in a pan with the potatoes, and remaining wormwood. Add water to cover, bring to the boil and simmer for about 15 minutes. Drain and remove the wormwood, then mash the potatoes and garlic. Press through a sieve, add salt and mix in 50 ml/2 fl oz of the remaining oil. Mix together the crème fraîche and the soft white cheese in a bowl.

Prepare the frogs' legs by removing the thigh bones and scraping the flesh away from the lower leg to expose the bone. One at a time, dip the frogs' legs in the crème fraîche mixture and then in the flour. Melt the butter in a nonstick pan. Fry the frogs' legs, turning them as soon as they begin to colour. When cooked through, transfer to a dish.

Heat the remaining oil and brown the goujonettes rapidly, then add salt and drizzle with lemon juice. Arrange them on plates. Shape the mashed potato into quenelles with tablespoons and place on the plates. Garnish with chive flowers.

Reheat the frogs' legs under a preheated grill and place on the plates around the potatoes. Spoon over the wormwood sauce and serve immediately.

Chef's tip The spicy, bitter flavour of the wormwood and the garlic enhance the taste of the frog meat. The chive flowers make this the perfect spring dish.

Scallops and tempura of young chicory seasoned with lemon balm and broom

Serves 4

Preparation time: 35 minutes
Cooking time: 15 minutes

Ingredients:

16 scallops
4 chicory heads, 44 leaves in total
125 ml/4 fl oz fresh lemon juice
25 g/1 oz butter, melted
1 teaspoon sugar, plus extra for the butter
1 bunch of lemon balm
2 tablespoons olive oil

2 shallots, finely chopped
100 ml/3½ fl oz white wine
100 ml/3½ fl oz milk
100 ml/3½ fl oz double cream
1 broom sprig
1 litre/1¾ pints oil, for deep-frying
salt
broom flowers, to garnish (optional)

Tempura batter:

50 g/2 oz plain flour
100 g/3½ oz potato flour
50 ml/2 fl oz white wine

Method:

Open the scallop shells with a sharp knife. Remove the scallop, skirt and coral. Separate them from the scallops, then rinse and drain. Place the scallops in the refrigerator, together with the coral and skirt, under a damp cloth.

Separate the chicory leaves. Cook in a large pan of salted water acidulated with a little lemon juice for 5 minutes, then refresh in cold water and drain. Coat with warm butter seasoned with a little sugar and salt (not to cook them but to give flavour). Layer 5 chicory leaves and some lemon balm leaves to form a millefeuille. Make 7 more millefeuilles and chill in the refrigerator.

Chop 25 g/1 oz of the remaining lemon balm. Heat half the olive oil in a pan. Add the scallop skirts and corals and the shallots and lightly brown. Pour in the wine and 100 ml/3½ fl oz water. Bring to simmering point, then add the chopped lemon balm, the remaining lemon juice, the sugar, milk, cream and salt. Return to a simmer for 5 minutes. Put 2 sprigs of lemon balm and the broom in a bowl and strain the mixture over them. Blend until smooth with a hand-held blender.

Heat the oil in a deep-fryer or large pan to 180–190°C/350°–375°F or until a cube of bread browns in 30 seconds. Mix all the batter ingredients with a little salt, 2 tablespoons water and 4 ice cubes. Dip

4 lemon balm leaves and the remaining 4 chicory leaves in the batter. One by one, immerse in the hot oil, then drain on kitchen paper.

Heat the remaining olive oil in a frying pan. Add the scallops and cook briefly on 1 side. Season with salt and turn on to a dish. The other side will finish cooking in the residual heat.

Warm up the chicory millefeuilles for 1 minute in a preheated oven, 180°C (350°F), Gas 4, or microwave.

Arrange 4 scallops, 2 millefeuilles, some tempura and sauce on each of 4 plates. Garnish with a sprig of lemon balm and, perhaps with some broom flowers, and serve immediately.

Chef's tip The citrus freshness of the lemon balm blends with the soft sweet flavour of the scallops. This is intensified by the sweet acidity of the broom, evocative of acacia, green lemons, hyacinth, narcissus and daffodils. A veritable bouquet of flowers. An excessive dose is known to slow the heartbeat. In the past, anyone who was unwilling to do military service would take broom before the medical examination and would subsequently be declared unfit for service. The chicory brings a touch of winter to these spring flavours.

Plum blossom in a basket and gratin of langoustines with sabayon sauce

Serves 4

Preparation time: 1 hour
Cooking time: 30 minutes

Ingredients:

20 langoustines
100 ml/3½ fl oz olive oil
1 carrot, cut into chunks
1 onion, cut into chunks
½ garlic bulb, peeled
1 leek, cut into chunks
50 ml/2 fl oz Cognac
400 ml/14 fl oz white wine

8 hibiscus flowers
1 plum tree sprig
1 teaspoon Sichuan pepper
100 ml/3½ fl oz mango juice
3 litres/5¼ pints oil, for deep-frying
4 egg yolks
salt and pepper
40 plum flowers, to garnish (optional)

Tempura batter:

50 g/2 oz plain flour
100 g/3½ oz rice flour
4 ice cubes
50 ml/2 fl oz white wine
2 tablespoons water
salt

Method:

Peel the langoustines, reserving the heads and shells. Heat 2 tablespoons of the oil and brown the heads and shells. Add a little more oil, then the carrot, onion, garlic and leek. Cook for  5 minutes over a high heat, then pour in the Cognac and ignite. When the flames have died down, pour in the white wine and 400 ml/14 fl oz water, bring to the boil and simmer for 30 minutes. Strain into a bowl, measure 250 ml/8 fl oz and add the hibiscus flowers, plum tree sprig and Sichuan pepper. Cover and leave to infuse for 10 minutes. Strain again and add the mango juice.

Heat the oil for deep-frying to 180–190°C/350–375°F or until a cube of bread browns in 30 seconds. Mix all the ingredients for the tempura batter. Stir in the plum tree blossom and mould into a 'basket' using 2 ladles. Immerse in the hot oil until golden, then drain on kitchen paper. Make 3 more baskets.

Heat the remaining olive oil. Fry the langoustines quickly on their backs, then remove from the pan.

Beat the egg yolks with the langoustine stock in a heatproof bowl. Set the bowl over a pan of barely simmering water and continue to beat until the sabayon sauce is frothy and increases in volume. Remove from the heat and season.

Pour the sabayon sauce into the bottom of the baskets, add the langoustines and brown for 1 minute under a preheated grill. Garnish with plum blossom, if you like, and serve.

Chef's tip Plum blossom tastes of almonds. Hibiscus gives the sabayon sauce a pretty pink colour, and its sour citrus flavour enhances the flavour of the langoustines. The mango and the Sichuan pepper leave a very slight aftertaste of fruit and spices. Dried hibiscus can be bought from a herbalist or health food store. In fact, health food stores sell many of the plants mentioned in these recipes.

Langoustines with confit of petit-gris snails and peas, coriander jus and young broad beans

Serves 4

Preparation time: 45 minutes
Cooking time: 8¼ hours

Ingredients:
12 langoustines, 3 kg/6½ lb
12 flat leaf parsley leaves
250 ml/8 fl oz white wine
4 garlic cloves
1 thyme sprig
2 bay leaves
20 petit-gris snails, starved

40 g/1½ oz peas, shelled
20 g/¾ oz butter
8 pinches of sugar
10 coriander seeds, crushed
1 bunch coriander
150 ml/¼ pint lamb or veal stock
(see page 185)
200 ml/7 fl oz red wine
40 g/1½ oz young broad beans, shelled
50 ml/2 fl oz olive oil
salt and pepper

Method:

Peel the langoustines, reserving 6 heads, and cut out the tiny black veins. Place a parsley leaf on each langoustine and set aside in the refrigerator.

Bring a pan of salted water to the boil and add 200 ml/7 fl oz white wine, the garlic, thyme and bay leaves. Add the snails and simmer for 6–8 hours.

Drain and reserve 6 tablespoons of the cooking liquid.

Remove the snails from their shells and trim. Set aside.

Place the peas in a deep frying pan. Add the butter, 4 pinches of sugar, salt and pepper. Cover with water and simmer until all the liquid has evaporated. Then add the snails.

Dry-fry the coriander seeds with 3 sprigs of fresh coriander in a frying pan. Add the stock, 5 tablespoons of the reserved cooking liquid, the red wine, the remaining white wine, the reserved langoustine heads, the remaining sugar, salt and pepper. Simmer gently for about 10 minutes, then strain over 3 sprigs of coriander.

Blanch the broad beans in boiling water for 30 seconds. Drain, refresh under cold water and skin.

Heat the olive oil in a frying pan and cook the langoustines quickly, only on the side with the parsley leaf. Season with salt, turn on to a dish and place in a preheated oven, 240°C (475°F), Gas Mark 9, for 1 minute. Warm the snail mixture until heated through. Reheat the broad beans in the remaining reserved cooking liquid.

Sprinkle 4 plates with the snail mixture and the broad beans. Arrange the langoustines in a fan, garnish with coriander leaves and serve.

Chef's tip The parsley leaves will become crisp on heating and will stick to the langoustines, creating a very decorative effect. I love the intense flavour of langoustines, which reminds me of properly hung meat. Coriander increases this meatiness, while introducing a slight sharpness. If any sauce is left over, you could mix it with a vinaigrette or a tomato stuffing, or even eat it cold with some bread and Brie. Leftovers inspire creativity. I like to combine sweet, sour and bitter flavours in my sauces. Sugar should not be obvious. It is only there to provide contrast. Quantities of salt and sugar should be in proportion. In general, I allow barely 3 parts sugar for 7 parts salt.

Risotto of spelt and clams with spices from the town of Apt

Serves 4

Preparation time: 45 minutes
Cooking time: 1 hour

Ingredients:
1 tablespoon olive oil
3 shallots, finely chopped
1 onion, finely chopped
1 teaspoon coriander seeds
2 kg/4 lb fresh clams, scrubbed

2 tablespoons Cognac
200 ml/7 fl oz white wine
1 bay leaf
140 g/4½ oz spelt
juice rind of 2 oranges
40 g/1½ oz butter
25 juniper berries
2 quarters of a candied orange, ideally
from the village of Apt
1 tablespoon sugar
12 cardamom leaves (optional)
100 ml/3½ fl oz fish stock (see page 185)
½ teaspoon cornflour
salt

Method:

Heat the olive oil in a pan and cook the shallots and onion over a low heat until softened. Add the coriander and the clams, then pour in the Cognac and ignite. When the flames die down, add half the white wine, the bay leaf and 300 ml/½ pint water. Cook over a high heat until the shells have all opened. Remove the clams with a slotted spoon, reserving the cooking liquid. Remove the clams from their shells, discarding any that remain shut.

Cook the spelt for 35 minutes in salted, boiling water. Drain and return to the pan with the reserved cooking liquid, half the orange juice, the butter and 6–7 juniper berries. Cover with water and simmer for about 20 minutes. The spelt should remain firm.

Cut the remaining juniper berries in half and the candied orange rind into pieces. Heat the sugar in a saucepan until caramelized. Add half the juniper berries, the cardamom leaves, if using, and candied orange rind. When a dark caramel has formed, stir in the remaining wine, the fish stock and the remaining orange juice, then simmer for 10 minutes. Stir the cornflour with 1 tablespoon cold water, then stir into the pan and simmer to thicken the sauce. Adjust the seasoning with salt, sugar and orange juice, if necessary. Strain over the remaining juniper berries. Shape the risotto into quenelles with 2 tablespoons, place on the plates and garnish with warm clams and sauce. Serve hot.

Chef's tip I prepare a vermicelli risotto in the same way, browned in olive oil like a rice pilaf, before drizzling with clam or fish stock and seasoning with juniper-flavoured caramel.

Skate wings poached in a vegetable stock, served over young leaves of New Zealand spinach in a sweet vinaigrette, seasoned with a coulis of oysters with lemon balm

Serves 4

Preparation time: 40 minutes

Cooking time: 15 minutes

Ingredients:

1 litre/1¾ pints vegetable stock
(see page 184)

4 skate wings with their black skin

750 g/1½ lb young New Zealand spinach
or garden spinach leaves, stalks removed
and thinly sliced

salt and pepper

Vinaigrette:

5 pink shallots, peeled

100 ml/3½ fl oz groundnut oil

50 ml/2 fl oz white wine vinegar

100 ml/3½ fl oz vegetable stock

1 teaspoon balsamic vinegar

Oyster coulis:

6 fresh oysters

2 pinches of sugar

4 tablespoons fresh lemon juice

5 lemon balm leaves

salt and pepper

Method:

Process all the vinaigrette ingredients in a blender or food processor.

Heat the vegetable stock with 500 ml/ 17 fl oz water and 25 g/1 oz salt. When it starts to simmer, add the skate wings and poach for 10 minutes without boiling. Leave to cool in the stock.

Open the oysters and drain and reserve the juices. Set them aside to produce some more juices, then combine that with the reserved juices.

Remove the oysters from their shells, and process with the reserved juices, the sugar, lemon juice, lemon balm and 3 ice cubes. Strain and season to taste with salt and pepper.

Dress the spinach leaves with the vinaigrette and arrange on a serving platter in a mound. Drain the skate wings. Remove and discard the skin, lift the flesh away from the cartilage using a spatula and arrange them like fans around the mounds of greens, placing them upside down to show the whitest part. Dress with the oyster coulis and serve immediately.

Chef's tip Skate wings need to be cooked slowly in order to preserve their delicate texture. The accompanying oyster coulis should be frothy, sweet-and-sour, extremely fresh, and should coat the fish. Sunflower buds, which were often cooked *à la barigoule*, that is, grilled, by our ancestors, can be used to impart a slight bitterness to this dish.

Fillet of exceptional grilled dentex, seasoned with candied orange and cade berries

Serves 4

Preparation time: 55 minutes
Cooking time: 30 minutes

Ingredients:

1 dentex or gilt-headed sea bream, about 1.25 kg/2½ lb, cleaned and scaled
100 ml/3½ fl oz olive oil
1 carrot, finely chopped,
1 onion, finely chopped
1 spring onion, finely chopped
1 bouquet garni
250 ml/8 fl oz white wine
50 g/2 oz butter
50 g/2 oz breadcrumbs
25 g/1 oz cade berries or juniper berries
25 g/1 oz candied orange peel
¼ teaspoon ground cardamom
1 teaspoon sugar
1½ teaspoons potato flour
juice of 1 orange
1 red oak leaf lettuce
200 g/7 oz mixed green salad and wild salad
3 tablespoons vinaigrette (see page 184)
sea salt, pepper

Method:

Remove the fillets from both sides of the fish and cut into thick chunks. Reserve the trimmings.

Heat 2 tablespoons of the olive oil in a pan and cook the fish bones over a low heat, then add the carrot, onion, spring onion and bouquet garni. Stir in 200 ml/ 7 fl oz of the wine and 200 ml/7 fl oz water and simmer very gently for 20 minutes, making sure that the stock does not become cloudy. Strain and set aside to cool completely.

Heat 2 tablespoons of the remaining oil with the butter and cook the breadcrumbs over a low heat, stirring until golden, glistening and crunchy. Using a large knife, thinly slice half the berries and half the orange peel. Place in a mortar with the cardamom and crush with a pestle, then mix with sea salt.

Cut the remaining berries in half and chop the remaining orange peel. Heat the sugar with a few drops of water until caramelized, then add the berries and orange peel.

Once a dark caramel has formed, stir in the remaining wine and 200 ml/7 fl oz of the cooled fish stock. Stir in the potato flour to thicken and season to taste with salt, more sugar, if necessary, and orange juice. Strain and keep warm in a bain-marie. Season the chunks of fish with salt and pepper, brush with oil and grill the skin side under a low heat. Sprinkle the uncooked side with some of the spiced breadcrumbs. Dress the salad leaves with the vinaigrette.

Arrange the fish and the salad on serving plates and drizzle with the sauce. Sprinkle with the remaining spiced breadcrumbs and serve.

Chef's tip Dentex is a member of the large sea bream family. It is found along the south coast of France and especially around Corsica. In Corsica, my stepfather and I go fishing for dentex among the rocks. There is no point trying to catch them in a net, as they will tear nets quite easily. It looks like a large gilt-headed bream and can reach a weight 15 kg/33 lb. We are able to buy beautifully plump candied oranges and their peel at markets, confectioners' and pâtisserie wholesalers. The town of Apt, situated at the base of the Luberon hills, is famous for its candied fruits. It is a real pleasure to go out in the fields and gather the various types of wild salad growing naturally each year. Don't be afraid to pick their flowers as well. Mix them with more traditional flowers, while capturing the wild spirit of young spinach leaves, oak leaf lettuce and young sorrel leaves.

Turbot braised in whey flavoured with vervain, and early rose potatoes crushed with lemon

Serves 4

Preparation time: 1 hour
Cooking time: 10 minutes

Ingredients:

1 turbot, about 1.5 kg/3 lb, cleaned
650 ml/23 fl oz whey, strained, or skimmed milk
12 early rose potatoes, unpeeled
2 lemon balm leaves, chopped
2 fennel sprigs, chopped
1 parsley sprig, chopped
1 sage leaf
1 marjoram sprig, chopped
2 basil leaves, chopped
4 tablespoons fresh lemon juice
25 g/1 oz butter
2 tablespoons crème fraîche
1 teaspoon olive oil
1 vervain plant
300 ml/½ pint asparagus cooking liquid
200 ml/7 fl oz fish stock (see page 185)
200 ml/7 fl oz single cream
2 pinches of sugar
salt and pepper

Method:

Cut the turbot in half lengthways, then into 4 thick steaks along its width. Place the steaks in the whey or milk and leave to stand to tenderize the flesh.

Cook the unpeeled potatoes in boiling water for 15–20 minutes. Peel and crush with a fork, together with the chopped herbs, lemon juice, 15 g/½ oz of the butter and the crème fraîche. Season with salt and pepper. Cover with clingfilm so that the mixture does not crust over and set aside but not in the refrigerator.

Drain the fish steaks, reserving 200 ml/7 fl oz of the marinade. Season the fish with salt and pepper on both sides. Melt the remaining butter with the oil in a frying pan. Add the fish, dark skin side down,.and cook until the skin is crisp., Turn and cook on the other side, then finish cooking over a low heat.

Reserve 4 vervain sprigs for garnish and place the vervain stems in a bowl. Mix the reserved marinade with the asparagus cooking liquid, fish stock and cream. Bring to the boil and reduce by half, then pour over the vervain stems, add the sugar and leave to infuse.

Arrange 1 turbot steak on each of 4 plates with a quenelle of crushed early rose potatoes and a vervain sprig. Blend the whey or milk mixture with a hand-held blender until frothy, then pour on to the plates and serve immediately.

Chef's tip Wild fennel, known as *fnu* in Provençal, has a crown of little yellow flowers and tastes like a mixture of caraway, dill and aniseed. Dill or caraway can be used in its place. I adore the smooth, almost buttery texture of early rose potatoes. They really do melt in the mouth. Even when they are very well cooked, they still taste very dry and floury. Alternatively, I use Monalisa potatoes which are also excellent.

Meat and poultry

Poultry • Guinea fowl from the Aix region, lacquered with coriander, with a vinaigrette of young vegetables from my garden • Chicken en vessie, with spelt and sweetcorn sauce flavoured with lemon balm • Sautéed saddle and poached shoulder of rabbit, turnips and spinach with milfoil and broom flowers • Seared pigeon and whey flavoured with rocket • **Beef** • Beef en croûte with a profusion of herbs and a light jus of mint • **Veal** • Veal chops, sautéed and braised, accompanied by onion compote and a buttery jus flavoured with chicory and roasted coffee • Veal kidneys with root vegetables, chicory leaves and flowers and Lourmarin grated potatoes • Calf's liver with beetroot and oregano • **Lamb** • Rillettes of lamb with caraway, or 'meadow cumin' • Rack of lamb smoked with wild thyme and my grandmother's gratin • Lamb shank confit and printanière of broad beans, with a light jus of bedstraw • **Pork** • Prime pork fat with oregano and cold grated Jerusalem artichoke • Pork loin with rue and rhubarb • Kromeskies of pig cheeks coated with hazelnuts, with an infusion of arquebus and St John's walnuts preserved in an 'old boy's jam' • Pig's trotters, tails and pork fillet, with curry plant • Pork fillet in a buck's horn plantain court-bouillon, with turnips and truffles

Guinea fowl from the Aix region, lacquered with coriander, with a vinaigrette of young vegetables from my garden

Serves 4

Preparation time: 45 minutes
Cooking time: 50 minutes

Ingredients:

½ bunch of coriander, plus 4 sprigs to garnish

2 free-range guinea fowls, halved

400 ml/14 fl oz white wine

750 g/1½ lb young vegetables (carrots with tops, turnips with tops, baby corn cobs, artichokes, mangetouts, grey chanterelles), chopped

6 carrots with tops, diced

4 cauliflower florets, diced

2 Jerusalem artichokes, diced

¼ celery stick, diced

1 fennel bulb, diced

1 tablespoon white wine vinegar

2 tablespoons olive oil

2 teaspoons orange juice

2 pinches of sugar

5 tablespoons vinaigrette (see page 184)

fine salt, sea salt flakes

Method:

Pick the coriander leaves from the stalks and chop half of them. Place the guinea fowls in a large, flameproof casserole, pour in the wine and add enough water to cover. Add the whole coriander leaves, season with salt and bring to the boil, then lower the heat and simmer for 6 minutes. Drain, reserving the cooking liquid and keep warm.

Poach all the young vegetables, except the mushrooms, in the reserved cooking liquid for about 15 minutes. Remove with a slotted spoon.

Add the carrots, cauliflower, artichokes, celery and fennel to the stock. Cook for 20 minutes, until the liquid has reduced, then blend with a hand-held blender and strain. Blend or whisk in the vinegar, oil, orange juice, chopped coriander, sugar and salt.

Carve the guinea fowl. Remove the wings, scraping the flesh from the tips of the wings to expose the bone. Slice the guinea fowl fillets finely, arrange on warm plates and coat with the vinaigrette of young vegetables.

Reheat the vegetables by steaming, in the microwave or in a pan with a little reserved stock. Divide the vegetables among the plates, add the raw chanterelles and coat with vinaigrette. Serve sprinkled with a few flakes of salt and garnished with coriander.

Chef's tip The flesh of the guinea fowl should be pink when cooked. My guests are often surprised by the flavour of raw grey chanterelles. They have a firm texture and slight taste of hazelnut, making them an excellent condiment (see also my recipe for Chilled 'agastache' soup and chanterelle mousseline with truffle oil on page 56).

Chicken en vessie, with spelt and sweetcorn sauce flavoured with lemon balm

Serves 4

Preparation time: 35 minutes

Cooking time: 1 hour

Ingredients:

400 g/14 oz spelt

1 bunch of lemon balm

2 free-range organic chickens, giblets removed, trussed with string

2 tablespoons olive oil

2 pigs' bladders

court-bouillon, for poaching

400 g/14 oz cooked sweetcorn

150 ml/¼ pint chicken stock (see page 184)

100 ml/3½ fl oz white wine

salt and pepper

4 tablespoons salted popcorn, to garnish

Method:

Cook the spelt in salted, boiling water for 40 minutes, until the grain bursts, drain and rinse with plenty of water. Pick the lemon balm leaves from the stalks. Stuff the chickens with spelt and a few lemon balm leaves.

Heat the olive oil in a frying pan and cook the chickens until golden brown all over, then place in separate bladders with the sweetcorn, salt and pepper. Inflate the bladders, seal and cook in a court-bouillon for 1 hour at 87–90°C/188–194°F (without boiling). Drain and open the bladders. Place the chickens on a dish and transfer the sweetcorn and cooking juices to a bowl. Scoop out the spelt from the chickens and remove some of the meat from the bones, pouring any juice into the sauce. Strain the cooking juices into a pan, reserving the sweetcorn. Add the stock and wine to the sauce, bring to simmering point and strain over the remaining lemon balm. Place the chicken carcasses and sweetcorn in the pan and leave to infuse. The sweetcorn will thicken the sauce. Shape the spelt into a circle on 4 plates (using a metal ring mould or by hand). Arrange some chicken meat on top and strain the sauce over. Garnish with lemon balm and popcorn.

Chef's tip Cooking in bladders produces extraordinary results. The flesh of the chickens is incredibly tender, the flavours are concentrated, and you can leave the meat to cook without any danger of its drying out. The spelt cooks to perfection inside the chickens, and the flavours of the meat, vegetables and sauce merge beautifully.

Sautéed saddle and poached shoulder of rabbit, turnips and spinach with milfoil and broom flowers

Serves 4

Preparation time: 1 hour
Cooking time: 45 minutes

Ingredients:
1 rabbit (see method)
3 milfoil sprigs
4 pinches of sugar
450 ml/¾ pint white wine
1 carrot, diced

½ leek, diced
2 onions, diced
1 clove
2 tablespoons olive oil
broom sprigs, plus 16 flowers
1 teaspoon cornflour
8 young round turnips
50 g/2 oz butter
400 g/14 oz spinach, stalks removed
(including 4 young leaves, raw)
salt and pepper

Method:

Ask your butcher to cut the shoulders and legs off the rabbit, and to remove the saddle carefully so that it does not tear. Ask him to give you the carcass, liver, kidneys and heart.

Pick the milfoil leaves from the stalks and reserve the flowers. Place 3 milfoil leaves in the middle of the saddle, season with salt and pepper and sprinkle lightly with sugar. Tie up with fine kitchen string or trussing thread.

Place the shoulders and legs of the rabbit in a deep frying pan, pour in the wine and add enough water to cover to twice the depth.

Add the carrot, leek, onions, clove, salt and pepper. Cover and simmer for about 30 minutes, then drain the meat, reserving the cooking liquid, and place in the refrigerator.

Crush the rabbit's carcass. Heat half the oil in a large pan and sauté the bones and offal. Pour in the reserved cooking liquid and cook over a medium heat for about 15 minutes, until reduced by half. Strain. Chop some of the broom sprigs and put them and the remaining milfoil in a pan and strain the sauce over. Leave to infuse for 5 minutes. Season with salt and pepper, remove the milfoil and return to the heat for 2 minutes. Mix the cornflour with a little water and stir into the sauce to thicken.

Cook the turnips in a large pan of salted, boiling water for 15 minutes.

Melt the butter in a pan, add the spinach and cook for 3 minutes.

Immediately remove from the pan and keep cool, in little bunches.

Heat the remaining olive oil. Brown the saddle on all sides. Transfer to a preheated oven, 220°C (425°F), Gas Mark 7, and cook for 5 minutes. Leave to stand for 5 minutes, then cut into 4 steaks.

Drain the turnips and cook quickly in the butter remaining in the spinach pan.

Place a leg or a shoulder, a saddle steak, a bunch of spinach and 2 turnips on each of 4 warm plates. Pour on the sauce and garnish with milfoil and broom flowers and raw spinach leaves before serving.

Chef's tip Milfoil is a plant with fine leaves, like dill, and little soft pink flowers which are very decorative. It has a slightly bitter flavour, which is why I add a little sugar to the saddle of rabbit. You can add a drop of white wine and a little sugar to the sauce to give it extra flavour. The saddle should be crusty and pink, and the turnips should melt in the mouth. Offer the legs to the gentlemen and the shoulders to the ladies. If you cannot find milfoil, you can use chrysanthemum, tansy, chamomile or even daisy leaves in its place.

Seared pigeon and whey flavoured
with rocket

Serves 4

Preparation time: 45 minutes

Marinating time: 12 hours

Cooking time: 20 minutes

Ingredients:

4 pigeons

150 ml/¼ pint single cream

3 tablespoons oil

200 g/7 oz rocket, plus 4 bunches of
rocket to garnish

25 g/1 oz butter

100 ml/3½ fl oz white wine

150 ml/¼ pint pigeon stock or chicken
stock with red wine (see page 184)

1 espresso coffee

½ teaspoon vinegar

150 ml/¼ pint whey or
skimmed milk

salt and pepper

Method:

Cut off the pigeon legs and detach each breast from the bone, leaving it attached to the wing. Reserve the carcasses. Place the legs and suprêmes in a dish, pour over the cream and marinate in the refrigerator for 12 hours.

Drain the pigeons reserving the cream, then place in a flameproof dish, skin side up, and season with fine salt.

Coat with cream marinade, reserving the remainder, and cook under a preheated grill for about 15 minutes, until the skin is crunchy and the flesh half-cooked. Remove from the grill and leave to cool during which time they will finish cooking. Season with salt and pepper. Heat the oil and brown the pigeon carcasses until the juices have caramelized. Remove the carcasses, add the rocket and butter to the pan and cook for 2 minutes. Add the white wine and then the stock, coffee, reserved cream, vinegar and whey or milk.

Cook over a medium heat for about 15 minutes, until reduced by about one-quarter. Blend with a hand-held blender and strain. Season with salt and pepper. Cut the pigeon suprêmes in half and arrange on 4 plates with the legs. If necessary, reheat under the grill.

Blend the rocket sauce again and pour on to the plates. Garnish each plate with a bunch of rocket and serve immediately.

Chef's tip In earlier years, I used to pick rocket on Mont Ventoux near Roussillon. These days I gather it in the vineyards, which are carpeted with white rocket flowers in spring. It spreads like wildfire over the freshly tilled soil. The bitterness of the coffee is reminiscent of red meat and enriches the flavour of the pigeon, while the cream marinade tenderizes its fibrous flesh. I accompany this dish with my grandmother Raymonde's potatoes au gratin (see page 104).

Beef en croûte with a profusion
of herbs and a light jus of mint

Serves 4

Preparation time: 1 hour

Cooking time: 40 minutes

Ingredients:

250 g/8 oz puff pastry, rolled out

1 bunch of marjoram, finely chopped

1 bunch of mint, finely chopped

1 bunch of savory, finely chopped

1 bunch of rosemary, finely chopped

20 g/¾ oz parsley, finely chopped

4 beef fillets, each weighing 150 g/5 oz

1 egg yolk

250 ml/8 fl oz vegetable stock
(see page 184)

250 ml/8 fl oz beef stock

250 ml/8 fl oz red wine

20 g/¾ oz coriander, finely chopped

1 star anise

1 teaspoon cornflour

salt and pepper

Method:

Cut out 4 fairly large rounds from the pastry. Place half each of the marjoram, mint, savory, rosemary and parsley in the middle of the pastry rounds, dividing them equally.

Season the beef fillets with salt and pepper, and arrange on top of the herbs. Wrap the pastry around the beef fillets to enclose them.

Glaze the pastry with egg yolk and cook in a preheated oven, 250°C (480°F), Gas Mark 10 or the highest setting, for 5 minutes. Pour the vegetable stock, beef stock and red wine into a saucepan, add the coriander and heat until reduced by about half.

Add the remaining herbs and star anise to the hot sauce, cover and leave to infuse for 7 minutes. Taste and, if necessary, adjust the seasoning.

Stir the cornflour with 1 tablespoon water, then stir into the sauce and cook until slightly thickened.

Reheat the fillets in the oven for 2 minutes, cut them in half and cover with the herb jus, strained if you like, before serving.

Chef's tip The combination of beef and carrots is engraved in our memory of flavours, and will always remind me of my grandmother's beef bourguignon. The classic combination of onion, garlic and carrots makes a great base for most dishes, especially beef, chicken and any other meat. It imparts structure to a dish, like salt and pepper. This is the reassuring aroma that floats in the stairwells of a building. I adore the classic sweetness of beef and carrots (I also prepare braised beef in autumn), but I prefer to combine these flavours with the herbs grazed by this beef cattle. Coriander reminds me of beef in the same way as red wine.

Veal chops, sautéed and braised, accompanied by onion compote and a buttery jus flavoured with chicory and roasted coffee

Serves 2

Preparation time: 30 minutes
Cooking time: 2 hours

Ingredients:
1 loin of veal, comprising 2 chops (see method)

5 onions, peeled
2 tablespoons olive oil
1 carrot, diced
½ leek, diced
3 garlic cloves, chopped
300 ml/½ pint white wine
1 teaspoon ground chicory
50 g/2 oz butter
chicory extract (optional)
1 espresso coffee
½ teaspoon cornflour
3 tablespoons gentian liqueur or eau de vie
6 chicory leaves and flowers
salt and pepper

Method:

Ask your butcher to tie up the veal loin and to save the crushed bones for you. Dice 1 onion.

Heat half the oil and brown the veal bone. Add the diced onion, carrot, leek and garlic and cook for 5 minutes. Pour in 200 ml/7 fl oz of the wine and 300 ml/ ½ pint water and simmer for 20 minutes, add the ground chicory and strain.

Season the remaining onions with salt and wrap separately in foil. Roast in a preheated oven, 120°C (250°F), Gas Mark ½, for 1 hour 20 minutes.

Heat the remaining oil with 20 g/¾ oz of the butter in a frying pan. Add the meat and cook until browned on 1 side. Season with salt and pepper, then brown the other side. Place the loin upright in a roasting tin and cook for 25 minutes in a preheated oven, 140°C (275°F), Gas Mark 1. Remove the meat from the tin and leave to stand for 8 minutes.

Caramelize the cooking juices over a high heat.

Add the remaining wine, the strained veal stock and espresso coffee. Mix the cornflour with 1 tablespoon water and stir in. Bring to the boil, stirring constantly. Taste and, if necessary, adjust the flavour with a little chicory extract. Stir in the gentian liqueur or eau de vie and whisk in the remaining butter.

Slice the loin into two chops. Arrange them with the cut surfaces facing upwards. Garnish with whole onions, with chicory leaves and flowers, and coat with sauce before serving.

Chef's tip This meat has a sweet, almost roasted flavour and its salty juices have a hint of milk which cries out for green vegetables such as peas and French beans. The roasted flavour and slight taste of toasted bread are combined here with bitter coffee to evoke the flavours of breakfast, hence the addition of chicory. You can improve the sauce by straining it over chicory roots (omit the gentian liqueur or eau de vie). Cooked slowly, this meat is absolutely bursting with juice and threatens to squirt everywhere when sliced. It is incredibly silky.

Veal kidneys with root vegetables, chicory leaves and flowers and Lourmarin grated potatoes

Serves 4–6

Preparation time: 1 hour
Cooking: time 1½ hours

Ingredients:

2 veal kidneys
8 potatoes
200 ml/7 fl oz double cream
2 tablespoons spelt flour or plain flour
2 eggs
1 teaspoon, plus 3 pinches of sugar
4 tablespoons olive oil
250 g/8 oz scrag end of veal, chopped
1 onion, diced
1 carrot, diced
½ leek, diced
3 garlic cloves, chopped

500ml/17 fl oz vegetable stock
(see page 184)
1 tablespoon ground chicory
1 bouquet garni (parsley, bay leaf, wild thyme, celery)
2 shallots, finely chopped
1 bay leaf
1 chicory root (optional)
5 tablespoons port
100 ml/3½ fl oz white wine
200 ml/7 fl oz whey or skimmed milk
1 tablespoon chicory extract
25 g/1 oz butter
500 ml/17 fl oz oil, for deep-frying
salt and pepper
chicory leaves and flowers dipped in vinaigrette (see page 184), to garnish

Method:

Core the kidneys and cut into small, even-size chunks, following the grain of the meat. Place in the refrigerator. Chop the trimmings and reserve. Grate the potatoes using a cheese grater, then squeeze between your hands to express the moisture. Mix with the cream, flour, eggs, 3 pinches of sugar and salt. Set aside in the refrigerator.

Heat 1 tablespoon of the oil and cook the kidney trimmings and veal until golden. Add the onion, carrot, leek and garlic and cook for 5 minutes. Add the stock, ground chicory and bouquet garni.

Cover and simmer for 1 hour, skimming occasionally. This should produce about 200 ml/7 fl oz veal stock.

Heat 1 tablespoon of the remaining oil and cook the shallots until golden. Add the bay leaf and chopped chicory root, if using. Cook until golden, then add the port and cook for 1 minute to reduce slightly. Pour in the wine, bring to the boil, then add the veal stock. Cook until reduced by half, then add the whey or skimmed milk. Season with salt and pepper, add the sugar and stir in the chicory extract to colour the sauce. Strain and keep warm in a bain-marie.

Heat 1 tablespoon of the remaining oil and cook the kidneys over a high heat. Season with salt and pepper. Transfer to a rack. Heat the remaining oil and fry the grated potatoes in 4 batches, a spoonful at a time, forming them into fritters. Drain immediately.

Before serving, place the kidneys in a preheated oven, 180°C (350°F), Gas Mark 4, for 2 minutes. Whisk the sauce with the butter. Arrange the kidneys in a semi-circle on plates, with 3 chicory leaves and flowers dipped in vinaigrette. Drizzle over the sauce at random. Serve the grated potatoes on the side.

Chef's tip I have been making these grated potatoes for many years, always with great success, and have dedicated them to Lourmarin. I never tire of the contrasting textures of the crunchy fritters and firm kidneys. You can decorate the plates with a bunch of chicory flowers. Chicory flowers from spring onwards and can be gathered in the hilly vineyards.

Calf's liver with beetroot and oregano

Serves 4

Preparation time: 20 minutes
Cooking time: 1 hour 40 minutes

Ingredients:
12 very small raw beetroots
875 g/1¾ lb calf's liver

2 tablespoons olive oil
50 ml/2 fl oz distilled white vinegar
2 pinches sugar
50 ml/2 fl oz white wine
50 ml/2 fl oz milk
25 g/1 oz butter
50 ml/2 fl oz single cream
1 bunch oregano, chopped
12 sorrel leaves or young spinach leaves
50 ml/2 fl oz vinaigrette (see page 184)
salt and pepper

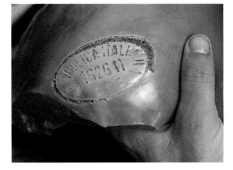 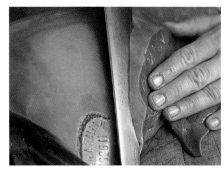 

Method:

Peel and trim the beetroots and reserve the trimmings in a pan.

Cook for 1 hour in salted, boiling water, until tender. Cut the calf's liver into 4 slices, about 200 g/7 oz each. Chop the liver trimmings and reserve.

Heat 1 tablespoon of the oil in a pan and brown the trimmings. Pour in the vinegar and cook until well reduced and nearly dry, as if you were making a béarnaise sauce. Add the sugar and wine and strain over the raw beetroot trimmings. Add the milk, butter and cream, bring to simmering point and cook for 5 minutes, then blend with a hand-held blender and strain over the oregano. Keep the sauce warm in a bain-marie; do not allow it to boil.

Taste the sauce and add more vinegar if it needs sharpening.

Heat the remaining oil and cook the liver on 1 side until browned. Place in a preheated oven, 150°C (300°F), Gas Mark 2, for 2 minutes. Season with salt and pepper.

Arrange the warm beetroot and sorrel or spinach leaves on 4 plates. Sprinkle with the vinaigrette, add the liver and sauce, then serve.

Chef's tip I like to slice liver into large steaks rather than the usual thin escalopes. Oregano complements liver as much as marjoram, but has a drier flavour. Beetroot has an earthy taste and gives the sauce an incredible fuchsia pink tint. In Savoie, beetroot collected in spring spends the winter in the bottom of the smokehouse, preserved by the humidity. This memory inspired me to create this recipe.

Rillettes of lamb with caraway, or 'meadow cumin'

Serves 4

Preparation time: 25 minutes

Cooking time: 3 hours

Chilling time: 1 hour

Ingredients:

1 kg/2 lb lamb panoufles (see Chef's tip)

1 bouquet garni (thyme, rosemary)

3 garlic bulbs, halved

100 ml.3½ fl oz white wine

50 ml/2 fl oz canned truffle juice

200 ml/7 fl oz olive oil

200 g/7 oz foie gras mousse

½ teaspoon ground cumin

15 g/½ oz parsley, chopped

salt and pepper

caraway flowers

Method:

Place the panoufles in a saucepan and add the bouquet garni, garlic and salt. Cover with water, bring to the boil and simmer for 3 hours.

Strain the stock through a sieve, then place in the refrigerator so that the fat solidifies. Place the meat in the refrigerator too.

When the fat has set, remove and reserve one-quarter of the fat. Process the meat in a food processor. Add the wine, truffle juice, olive oil, reserved lamb fat, foie gras mousse, cumin, chopped parsley, salt and pepper and mix well.

Divide the mixture among individual dishes or form into a sausage and wrap in foil. Chill in the refrigerator.

Serve very cold, with croûtons, cutting the 'sausage' into slices.

Chef's tip Lamb reminds me of Provence and the Hautes-Alpes and is my favourite meat. It has an addictive flavour, like pasta. I enjoy lamb hot or cold, savoury or sweet. Its milky flavour is not quite that of meat. It is closer to veal, though slightly more acidic. I like lamb blended with butter and spread on bread, so I created these rillettes which are cooked slowly in stock. Lamb can be very dry or very juicy, depending on how it is cooked. Panoufles are the upper part of the chops (the fatty bit). This cut is usually discarded, but is wonderful when prepared in this way. Port can be used in place of truffle juice.

Rack of lamb smoked with wild thyme and my grandmother's gratin

Serves 4

Preparation time: 1 hour
Cooking time: 45 minutes

Ingredients:
3 garlic bulbs
200 g/7 oz butter
1 kg/2 lb potatoes, thinly sliced
1 leek, diced
1 bouquet garni, consisting of thyme,
rosemary and bay leaf

2 litres/3½ pints milk
50 g/2 oz grated Gruyère cheese
125 ml/4 fl oz crème fraîche
1 large bunch of wild thyme
100 g/3½ oz streaky bacon
2 racks of lamb,
each comprising 6–8 chops
500 ml/17 fl oz vegetable stock
(see page 184)
150 g/5 oz plain flour
½ teaspoon coarse salt
fine salt, pepper

Method:

Reserve 4 garlic cloves for the garnish, then peel and chop the remainder. Melt the butter in a pan and gently cook the garlic without colouring. Add the potatoes, leek, bouquet garni, salt and pepper. Pour in the milk and simmer for 20 minutes, until the potatoes are tender. Divide the potatoes among 4 ramekins. Sprinkle with Gruyère, cover with crème fraîche and add a sprig of wild thyme and an unpeeled garlic clove to each. Cook in a preheated oven, 220°C (425°F), Gas Mark 7, for about 10 minutes.

Cook the streaky bacon in a nonstick pan over high heat until the fat runs.

Add the racks of lamb and cook over a high heat for 5 minutes. Season with salt and pepper, then set aside. Pour off the fat, reserving the bacon. Stir the stock into the pan and cook over a high heat for 10 minutes, or until reduced by about a quarter. Strain. Place the lamb racks in a casserole and cover with the remaining wild thyme. Dice the streaky bacon and sprinkle it on top.

Mix the flour with 50 ml/2 fl oz water and the coarse salt to make a paste. Roll into a long sausage and use to seal the lid on to the casserole. Cook in a preheated oven, 250°C (480°F), Gas Mark 10 or at the highest setting, for 10 minutes.

Break the seal and open the casserole in front of your guests. Accompany with little ramekins of potatoes au gratin.

Chef's tip When you open the casserole in front of your guests, the aroma of wild thyme and lamb will fill the room. Wild thyme is common on the scrublands of Provence. I gather it among the stones and fallen rocks of the Claparèdes, on the ground riddled with anthills. I love its vibrancy and the subtle lemon flavour. Milder in flavour than the garden variety, wild thyme is reminiscent of moss and humid soil. Its flowers last until August.

Lamb shank confit and printanière of broad beans, with a light jus of bedstraw

Serves 4

Preparation time: 35 minutes
Cooking time: 30 minutes

Ingredients:
500 ml/17 fl oz lamb stock
¼ leek, thinly sliced
1 rosemary sprig
2 onions, finely chopped
150 g/5 oz sesame seeds
3 star anise

1 caraway leaf or a few cumin seeds
4 lamb shanks
2 tablespoons oil
1 teaspoon sugar
½ teaspoon cornflour
8 bedstraw flowers
100 ml3½ fl oz red wine
200 g/7 oz broad beans,
shelled and peeled
2 savory sprigs
25 g/1 oz butter
salt

Method:

Pour the stock into a steamer or couscoussier. Add the leek, rosemary, 1 onion, 100 g/3½ oz of the sesame seeds, the star anise and caraway leaf.

Expose the bone at the top of the lamb shanks by scraping away the flesh. Trim the bases so that they stand upright and reserve the trimmings. Season with salt and steam the meat for 12 minutes. Leave the lamb to stand. Strain the stock. Heat 1 tablespoon of the oil and cook the remaining onion until translucent, then sprinkle with the sugar and cook until caramelized. Stir in 300 ml/½ pint of the strained stock. Mix the cornflour with 1 tablespoon water, stir into the pan and bring to the boil, stirring to thicken. Add the bedstraw flowers.

Chop the lamb trimmings. Heat the remaining oil and cook the trimmings with the remaining sesame seeds. Add the wine and then pour into the sauce.

Cook the broad beans in boiling water for 5–10 minutes, then drain. Melt the butter in a pan and braise the broad beans with the savory for 3 minutes, then deglaze with a little water.

Spread the broad beans on 4 plates. Stand the lamb shanks upright on this bed of beans, cover with sauce and serve.

Chef's tip Bedstraw has yellow flowers in the shape of an elongated pompom, like an asparagus head. It can be gathered along the arid paths of Provence from mid-spring to the beginning of summer. The fragrance of this flower is reminiscent of honey and beehives, hinting at rich stores of pollen and nectar. It has a herbal flavour similar to broom and combines well with the soft sweetness of lamb and sourness of broad beans. If you cannot find bedstraw, you could use a few drops of hazelnut oil in its place.

Prime pork fat with oregano and cold grated Jerusalem artichoke

Serves 4

Preparation time: 30 minutes

Salting time: 24 hours

Cooking time: 25 minutes

Ingredients:

875 g/1¾ lb prime pork fat (see Chef's tip)

1 tablespoon coarse salt

300 ml/½ pint white wine

1 carrot, cut into chunks

1 onion, cut into chunks

1 leek, cut into chunks

1 clove

pinch of grated nutmeg

1 bay leaf

1 bunch of oregano, plus oregano flowers

4 Jerusalem artichokes

4 tablespoons fresh lemon juice

50 ml/2 fl oz olive oil

150 g/5 oz soft white cheese

fine salt, pepper

Method:

Sprinkle the pork fat with the coarse salt and leave to stand for 24 hours at room temperature.

Next day, rinse the pork fat in cold water and place in a pan with the wine, carrot, onion, leek, clove, nutmeg, bay leaf and 1 sprig of oregano. Add water to cover, bring to the boil and simmer for 15 minutes. Using a slotted spoon, transfer the pork fat to a plate and leave to stand for 15 minutes to soften, then slice it thinly.

Peel and grate the Jerusalem artichokes. Mix with the lemon juice, oil, cheese, salt and pepper, then divide the mixture among 4 plates. Garnish with slices of pork fat and oregano flowers and petals before serving with bread.

Chef's tip I adore the prime fat of free-range pork. We are not talking about the flabby fat which clings to the flesh of intensively reared pigs. Eaten raw, this fat is firm and tasty. It is sliced finely like ham, and can be dried. When cooked, it retains its firm texture and yields little fat. I like it warm and tender, almost jellified, but you can also chill it to make it firmer. Its beautiful pearly colour blends with the white Jerusalem artichokes, creating a white backdrop tinged with pink. The only contrast is provided by the little purple flowers of the oregano, which add a sour earthy note to the crisp lemony salad. This salad is similar to my celery remoulade.

Pork loin with rue and rhubarb

Serves 4	2 bay leaves
	1 pork loin, comprising 4 chops
Preparation time: 45 minutes	1 teaspoon vinegar
Cooking time: 10 minutes	1 teaspoon cornflour
Standing time: 10 minutes	300 g/10 oz sugar
	4 rhubarb sticks
Ingredients:	40 g/1½ oz butter
1 onion, diced	2 late winter quinces, sliced
1 garlic clove, chopped	1 tablespoon olive oil
1 tomato, diced	1 teaspoon clear honey
1 bunch of rue	salt and pepper
500 ml/17 fl oz white wine	

Method:

Put the onion, garlic, tomato, 1 sprig of rue, the wine, bay leaves and 500 ml/ 17 fl oz water into a heavy pan. Bring to the boil. Add the pork loin and simmer for 4 minutes. Drain, reserving the stock, and cool, then transfer the meat to the refrigerator.

Chop the remaining rue and place in a heatproof bowl. Boil the stock for 10 minutes, then season with vinegar, salt, pepper and a few pinches of sugar. Mix the cornflour with a little cold water, then stir into the stock. Cook over a high heat, stirring constantly, until thickened, then strain over the rue. Keep warm in a bain-marie.

Remove the leaves from the rhubarb and trim. Cut the sticks into 5 cm/2 inch lengths, then slice in half lengthways. Roll in the remaining sugar and leave to release their juices, then remove from the sugar. Melt 25 g/1 oz of the butter and cook the rhubarb briefly. Add salt and a drop of water.

Melt the remaining butter and cook the quinces until caramelized. Heat the oil in another pan and brown the skin side of the pork loin. Transfer to an ovenproof dish, brush with the honey and place in a preheated oven, 220°C (425°F), Gas Mark 7, for 1 minute. Slice into chops, arrange on plates with the rhubarb, coat with sauce and serve.

Chef's tip Pork reminds me of veal in terms of cooking methods. The male pig or boar is not used in cookery, since it has an unattractive smell of urine. I try to recreate this acidic aroma in young pork by combining it with white wine and herbs which taste slightly fermented, such as santolina, wormood or caraway (wild cumin). Pork also needs acidity (provided by the rhubarb) and caramelized sweetness (quince). Finally, pepper is needed to harmonize the combination of meat and the sweet-and-sour flavour. Cooking the loin in this way preserves the flavour of the pork. The caramelized skin contrasts with the tender milky flesh, almost like white butter, enhanced here by the rhubarb juice. Quince improves with age and does not deteriorate at all when dried. I hang quince around my house so that the aroma fills every room. Rue has a slightly peppery taste similar to Sichuan pepper. If you cannot find rue, use plenty of pepper.

Kromeskies of pig cheeks coated with hazelnuts, with an infusion of arquebus and St John's walnuts preserved in an 'old boy's jam'

Serves 4

Preparation time: 55 minutes
Cooking time: 2 hours 10 minutes

Ingredients:
750 g/1½ lb pig cheeks
1.3 litres/2¼ pints white wine
12 green walnuts
50 g/2 oz sugar, plus extra for the walnuts

10 arquebus or tarragon sprigs
100 g/3½ oz foie gras mousse
50 g/2 oz plain flour
3 eggs, lightly beaten
200 g/7 oz hazelnuts, crushed
100 ml/3½ fl oz single cream
50 ml/2 fl oz milk
50 ml/2 fl oz white wine vinegar
500 ml/17 fl oz oil, for deep-frying
fine salt, pepper

Method:

Place the pig cheeks in a large pan. Reserve 125 ml/4 fl oz of the wine and pour the remainder into the pan. Add enough salted water to cover the meat. Bring to the boil and poach for 2 hours. Cook the green walnuts with some sugar in boiling water, then drain and reserve. Reserve 4 herb sprigs for garnish. Chop the remainder, keeping the leaves and stalks separate.

Drain the pig cheeks, reserving 100 ml/3½ fl oz of the cooking liquid. Mince the meat in a bowl, adding 1 tablespoon of the reserved wine, the foie gras mousse and half the chopped herb leaves. Season with salt and pepper, and mix well. Make 12 balls of this mixture and roll each ball first in the flour, then the beaten eggs and, finally, the hazelnuts.

Heat the remaining white wine in a pan until reduced by half. Add the reserved stock, chopped herb stalks, cream, milk and 2 tablespoons of the vinegar. Bring to the boil and add a little salt and the sugar. Strain over the remaining chopped herbs and keep warm in a bain-marie.

Heat the oil to 160°C/325°F or until a cube of stale bread browns in 45 seconds. Deep-fry the kromeskies, then drain on kitchen paper.

Heat the walnuts in the oven with the remaining vinegar.

Strain the sauce again and adjust the seasoning. It should be slightly acidic.

Divide the kromeskies and walnuts among 4 large plates and decorate each plate with 1 herb sprig. Blend the sauce with a hand-held blender until smooth, then pour between the walnuts and kromeskies. Serve immediately.

Chef's tip 'Old boy's jam' is made on 24 June, the feast day of St John, three days after the summer solstice. The walnuts are still green, giving them a distinctive, slightly sour taste.

Pig's trotters, tails and pork fillet, with curry plant

Serves 4	4 pigs' tails
	1 pork fillet
Preparation time: 1 hour	50 g/2 oz butter
Cooking time: 1¼ hours	2 pinches sugar
	200 ml/7 fl oz milk
Ingredients:	250 ml/8 fl oz crème fraîche
1 carrot	1 bunch of curry plant sprigs and flowers
2 onions	4 pinches cornflour
1 leek, green leaves only	4 pinches cumin powder
3 ribs of Swiss chard	4 pinches curry powder
250 ml/8 fl oz white wine	1 skinless chicken breast fillet, chopped
½ nutmeg, grated	1 egg
2 cloves	3 tablespoons port
1 bay leaf	1 piece of caul fat or 6–8 bacon rashers
4 juniper berries	1 tablespoon olive oil
3 pigs' trotters	salt and pepper

Method:

Put the carrot, 1 onion, the leek and Swiss chard in a large pan with the wine, 250 ml/8 fl oz water, the nutmeg, cloves, bay leaf, juniper berries and salt. Add the pigs' trotters and tails. Bring to the boil, then simmer for 15 minutes. Remove the tails and continue to simmer the trotters for 25 minutes, topping up with water if necessary. Leave to cool. Remove the flesh from the trotters and place in the refrigerator with the carrot and leek. Reserve the stock.

Trim the pork fillet, reserving the trimmings. Melt 25 g/1 oz of the butter and cook the fillet for 5 minutes.

Dice the remaining onion and the pork trimmings. Heat the remaining butter with the sugar and cook the onion and pork trimmings until caramelized. Pour in the reserved stock and cook over a high heat until reduced by half, then pour in the milk and 200 ml/7 fl oz of the crème fraîche and simmer for 5 minutes. Add the curry plant sprigs, reserving the flowers, and infuse for 5 minutes. Season with pepper. Mix the cornflour with a little cold water and stir in. Cook over a medium heat for a further 2 minutes to thicken the sauce, then strain and season with cumin and curry powder.

Mix together the chopped chicken, egg, the remaining crème fraîche and the port. Cut the pigs' trotters, carrot and leek into tiny cubes. Combine with the chicken mixture and half the curry plant flowers. Roll into 4 balls and wrap with caul fat or stretched bacon to form crépinettes.

Heat the oil in a nonstick pan. Cook the pigs' tails and crépinettes without allowing them to touch. Finish cooking in a preheated oven, 180°C (350°F), Gas mark 4, for 10 minutes.

Place 1 pig's tail, 3 slices of fillet and 1 crépinette, golden side up, on each of 4 plates. Drizzle with the sauce, garnish with curry plant flowers and serve.

Chef's tip This dish is inspired by the traditional combination of pork and curry. It uses three different cooking methods for three different cuts. The gristly trotters, crusty tails and tender pink fillet leave contrasting sensations in the mouth. The accompanying pork gravy contains curry plant and adds a peppery note to the dish, mellowed by the addition of milk and cream. This flower belongs to the family of golden germanders and produces beautiful yellow flowers shaped like little bells. It can be found in the Corsican maquis and all along the Mediterranean coast.

Pork fillet in a buck's horn plantain court-bouillon, with turnips and truffles

Serves 4

Preparation time: 30 minutes

Cooking time: 30 minutes

Ingredients:

2 fillets of pork

500 ml/17 fl oz white wine

12 turnips, peeled with tops reserved

25 g/1 oz butter

2 tablespoons olive oil

3 tablespoons port

3 tablespoons Cognac

100 ml/3½ fl oz canned truffle juice

100 g/3½ oz buck's horn plantain

4 truffles, each 25 g/1 oz

salt and pepper

Method:

Trim the pork fillets, reserving the trimmings.

Bring the wine and 500 ml/17 fl oz water to simmering point, together with the pork trimmings and turnip tops. Season with salt. Add the turnips and cook for about 15 minutes.

Heat the butter with the oil and cook the pork fillets until golden on all sides.

Transfer to a preheated oven, 220°C (425°F), Gas Mark 7, for 4 minutes. Leave the meat to stand on a plate for 4 minutes. Stir the port, Cognac, truffle juice and stock into the pan to deglaze. Reduce for 5 minutes over a high heat. Slice the fillets and place on plates with the turnips and a bouquet of buck's horn plantain. Pour over the sauce, cover with thin slices of truffle and serve.

0Chef's tip Ever loyal to my grandmother's principles, I cook all vegetables until they are beautifully tender. The turnips should melt in the mouth. Turnips and buck's horn plantain have an earthy taste which is amplified here by truffles. *Tuber melanosporum* are very expensive in spring, so I use the *ostinatum* variety of truffle at this time of year. This variety is distinguished primarily by its half-white half-grey colour, its larger spores and its crisp texture. The pork juices have a slight acidity which I balance with the sweetness of the reduced port and cooked turnips. This dish can be garnished with yellow buck's horn plantain flowers. Mustard or rocket leaves can be used instead.

Germination – the plants burst into life

Above:
Fresh, rich soil
ensures a thick, bushy growth.

Édouard and Adrien make their compost from the detritus of plants; they then pile it into a hole in the garden where it develops into a superb natural humus, rich in nitrates. It needs time – a year, maybe two – but it is very effective. Even so, snow remains the best fertilizer. In a poor year, gardeners may resort to using a nitrate additive.

Merely nourishing the soil, however, is not enough; it needs raking and turning over, especially in spring and just before the early frosts. This helps it to retain moisture – as the saying goes, 'One hoeing is worth three waterings'. Without adequate aeration, the soil will become airtight and depleted.

After the plough, its time to harrow the soil to break up the clods of earth, then to rake and smooth it in preparation for the new seeds. If necessary, it can also be enriched with the addition of nitrates and fertilizer. Finally, it is covered with a layer of manure. As soon as the soil is ready, it is time for sowing; thus the cycle continues... 'The ox may be slow but the land is patient,' remarks Édouard philosophically. Between mid-February and mid-March everything slowly develops and, at last, plants start to emerge: baby spinach, baby turnips, radishes, daffodils. Germination is a new beginning, the renewal of life on barren ground – a green shoot sprouting from a shrivelled onion.

Most small plants are grown from seed, a riot of millions of seedlings – of chive or strawberry, for instance – which are transplanted into regular, well-spaced rows. Next come the beans, radishes, spinach, Swiss chard, parsley, hyssop and tarragon, which do not need to be transplanted. They are picked as they appear. Salad vegetables grow freely, like a lawn,

In the fields, the wheat is 5 cm/2 inches high. It is now or never for Édouard to make his famed *jus de blé vert centrifuges* – pressed juice of green wheat.

Opposite:
Vines resume their annual cycle
of growth; cherry trees in
well-tended soil await the revival
of spring.

Vegetables

Barigoule of violet artichokes, and mousseline of sea squirts with a hint of wax • Burnet and milfoil salad • Green asparagus from Villelaure, savory cream and sea urchin butter • Freshly gathered flowers, onion confit and truffles • Fried morels with liquorice root • Printanière of morels with salt crust and ground ivy, smoked with cedar • Sunflower hearts with sweet vinaigrette, grated potato fritters and chanterelles with a lovage gazpacho • Asparagus flan with hazelnuts, quail's eggs and praline sauce

Barigoule of violet artichokes, and mousseline of sea squirts with a hint of wax

Serves 4

Preparation time: 1 hour
Cooking time: 20 minutes

Ingredients:

26 violet artichokes
125 ml/4 fl oz lemon juice
300 ml/½ pint olive oil
2 carrots, finely diced
1 onion, finely diced
2 slices of smoked ham, finely diced
1 bay leaf

10 juniper berries
8 coriander seeds
1 clove
1 potato, peeled
½ teaspoon sugar
1 litre/1¾ pints white wine
200 g/7 oz butter
250 ml/8 fl oz vinegar
10 raw sea squirts, shelled
1 garlic clove
2 egg yolks
salt and pepper
8 grey chanterelle mushrooms, to garnish
4 slices of rustic bread, to serve

Method:

Remove the leaves from the artichokes and peel the stalks (which are also very tender and tasty), then place in water mixed with 4 tablespoons lemon juice to prevent them from discolouring.

Heat 50 ml/2 fl oz of the olive oil in a saucepan and cook the carrots, onion and ham over a low heat. Add the bay leaf, juniper, coriander seeds, clove, potato and drained artichokes. Season with salt, pepper and sugar, pour in the wine and add the butter and vinegar. Season again with salt and pepper, cover and simmer for 20 minutes. Empty the contents of the pan into a bowl, setting aside 10 artichokes and the potato.

Purée the reserved potato and artichokes with the sea squirts, garlic, salt and pepper. Mix in the egg yolks and the remaining lemon juice, then whisk in the remaining olive oil like an aïoli.

Garnish with raw chanterelles and serve the dish cold, with slices of bread and the artichoke mousseline.

Chef's tip Violet artichokes have a slight taste of wax which lends itself well to this method of cooking *en barigoule*. This is a typical Provençal recipe, which I have garnished with an artichoke aïoli. This sauce could be improved further by mixing with some of the cooking stock. Accompany this dish with a generous spoonful of goat's cheese flavoured with chopped hyssop.

Burnet and milfoil salad

Serves 4

Preparation time: 20 minutes

Cooking time: 25 minutes

Ingredients:

200 g/7 oz shelled peas

5 spinach leaves, stalks removed

100 ml/3½ fl oz vinaigrette (see page 184)

100 g/3½ oz milfoil, leaves removed

100 g/3½ oz salad burnet, leaves removed

Édouard prepares the milfoil

Method:

Cook the peas in salted, boiling water for 20 minutes, then purée with a hand-held blender and press through a sieve. Shred the spinach leaves, then mix them into the peas with 3 tablespoons of the vinaigrette to form a thick paste.

Season the milfoil and salad burnet with vinaigrette to taste. Divide the pea mixture among 4 dishes, garnish with domes of salad and serve cold.

Chef's tip This book is a tribute to the gardeners, farmers and cooks who combine science and patience. In our garden, we grow unusual herbs and rare vegetables, including seakale, gumbo and asparagus beans, and cultivate them organically with natural pesticides, such as infusions of walnut and tobacco leaves or even diluted soap. It is possible to fill your flowerbeds with plants which are both decorative and delicious: elegant umbelliferae, roses, cardoon flowers, tansy and red chard. Why not grow castor oil plants and currants among your asparagus? Don't forget to include chicory and liquorice for their spicy leaves and glorious flowers. Another elegant plant is milfoil, which has an astringent earthy flavour similar to peas. Salad burnet has a slight aftertaste of flour and chestnuts. These three elements blend perfectly in this recipe.

Green asparagus from Villelaure, savory cream and sea urchin butter

Serves 4–6

Preparation time: 45 minutes
Cooking time: 1 hour

Ingredients:

2 bunches of asparagus, peeled
3 tablespoons olive oil
36 sea urchins
1 thyme sprig, chopped
1 bay leaf
1 onion, chopped

1 carrot, chopped
3 garlic cloves, crushed
10 coriander seeds, crushed
dash of Armagnac
250 ml/8 fl oz white wine
1 tablespoon tomato purée
750 ml/1¼ pints single cream
150 g/5 oz butter, diced
juice of 2 oranges
4 tablespoons fresh lemon juice
3 tablespoons chopped savory
2 teaspoons sugar
5 teaspoons distilled white vinegar
salt and pepper

Method:

Gather the asparagus into a bunch, tie at both ends and cook in very salty, boiling water for 10–15 minutes. Check to see if it is tender by inserting the point of a knife. Drain the asparagus, untie and refresh in a bowl of iced water. Cut off and reserve the tips of each spear.

Prepare the sea urchin bisque. Heat the olive oil in a flameproof casserole over a high heat. Add 30 sea urchins and the thyme, bay leaf, onion, carrot, garlic and coriander seeds. Crush the sea urchins with a pestle while continuing to sear them over the heat.

Stir in the Armagnac and wine to deglaze and bring to the boil, then stir in the tomato purée. Add 1 litre/1¾ pints water and simmer until reduced by half. Add half the cream and cook for 15 minutes more. Process in a food processor or blender, strain and adjust the seasoning. The bisque should be slightly peppery. Gradually add the butter and blend with a hand-held blender.

Prepare the savory cream. Mix together the orange and lemon juice, savory, 1 teaspoon salt and the sugar. Whisk the remaining cream in a separate bowl until firm, then stir in the citrus juice mixture and, finally, the vinegar. The cream should be sweet-and-sour. Chill.

Open the remaining sea urchins by cutting around the mouths using scissors. Drain their juice and place a sea urchin on each plate, next to a pile of asparagus tips and quenelles of savory cream.

Blend the bisque with a hand-held blender until frothy, pour on to the plates, add a few grains of salt and serve.

Chef's tip Keep your raw asparagus fresh for several days by placing the stalks in water (this is what the producers do) and storing in the refrigerator. Add salt to the cooking water as it starts to boil, then drop in the asparagus. The salt sets the chlorophyll and contributes to the green colour. Always the good farmer, I never throw away the trimmed ends of the asparagus. You can always purée them and add to a vinaigrette, for example.

Freshly gathered flowers, onion confit and truffles

Serves 4

Preparation time: 20 minutes
Cooking: time 25 minutes

Ingredients:
4 Simiane onions
125 g/4 oz butter

4 tablespoons honey
4 juniper berries
4 truffles
50 g/2 oz wild chicory or endive,
finely chopped
50 g/2 oz wild turnips or young turnips
with tops, finely chopped
1 small bunch of radishes, finely chopped
50 g/2 oz sunflowers, finely chopped
100 ml/3½ fl oz vinaigrette (see page 184)
salt

Method:

Place the onions in a high-sided frying pan that can safely be put in the oven, together with the butter, honey, juniper and salt. Add water to cover and bring to simmering point, then cover the pan with foil and finish cooking in a preheated oven, 180°C (350°F), Gas Mark 4, for 20 minutes. Remove from the oven and leave to cool. Brush the truffles and slice thinly. Combine the chicory or endive, turnips, radishes and sunflowers and toss with the vinaigrette. Garnish with the onions, sprinkle with slices of truffle and serve immediately.

Chef's tip In Provence, we eat wild chicory, wild turnips, radishes and sunflowers just like the thrushes. This selection of wild salads can be garnished with lamb's lettuce, salsify flowers, dandelion and all the succulent young shoots of early spring, such as the first oak leaf lettuces (crisp and bitter), chives and clover flowers (beautifully sweet at the beginning of the season). The most sumptuous feasts can be prepared from the humblest ingredients. This elegant dish is based on freshly gathered salad and a handful of onions. In Provence, this is a 'poor man's salad' as anyone can go out and gather these herbs and truffles. Finish with a soft-boiled egg, some croûtons and a drop of truffle oil. If you cannot find any sunflowers, you can use young turnip or radish leaves instead.

Fried morels with liquorice root

Serves 4

Preparation time: 55 minutes
Cooking time: 25 minutes

Ingredients:

32 fresh morel mushrooms
150 g/5 oz butter
200 g/7 oz dried morel mushrooms
3 shallots, unpeeled and finely chopped
100 g/3½ oz celeriac, diced
3 bay leaves

2 cloves
4 tablespoons Cognac
150 ml/¼ pint white wine
1 stock cube
200 ml/7 fl oz single cream
100 ml/3½ fl oz milk
½ teaspoon cornflour
2 sticks of liquorice, cut into thin batons
3 tablespoons lemon juice
3 pinches of sugar
4 teaspoons white wine vinegar (optional)
salt and pepper

Method:

Peel the fresh morel stalks, reserving the trimmings. Melt 15 g/½ oz of the butter, season with salt and pepper and use to coat the morels.

Place the dried morels in a bowl, add water to cover and leave to soak. Melt 15 g/½ oz of the remaining butter in a pan and cook the shallots, celeriac and morel trimmings until slightly caramelized. Drain the rehydrated mushrooms, reserving the soaking liquid. Add them to the pan and cook for 5 minutes. Add the bay leaves, cloves, 3 tablespoons of the Cognac, 100 ml/3½ fl oz of the wine, half the stock cube, half the cream and the milk. Season with salt and pepper.

Flavour the sauce with 5 tablespoons of the reserved mushroom soaking liquid. Bring the mixture to the boil. Mix the cornflour with 1 tablespoon water, then stir into the pan. Bring back to the boil, gradually whisk in 100 g/3½ oz butter and add the remaining Cognac. Keep warm in a bain-marie.

Heat the remaining butter and cook one-third of the liquorice. Crumble in the rest of the stock cube and add the remaining wine, the lemon juice, sugar, salt and pepper. Stir in the remaining cream and simmer gently for 5 minutes. Place half the remaining liquorice in a bowl, strain the mixture over it and leave to infuse. Taste and adjust the sweet-and-sour flavour with vinegar, if necessary.

Fry the morels on one side so that one side is crusty and the other is almost raw. Drizzle the morel sauce on 4 plates, add the mushrooms and garnish with the remaining liquorice batons. Pour 1 tablespoon of liquorice sauce on one side and serve.

Chef's tip Morels are complemented by spicy flavours such as liquorice. At the restaurant, I garnish this dish with liquorice root, which I shred and boil before frying with the morels. Liquorice grows in damp undergrowth, among the moss, soil and stones. Fresh liquorice root has a sticky sweet flavour rather like an unripe almond, with a hint of earth and lichen, and the crunchy texture of bamboo.

Printanière of morels with salt crust and ground ivy, smoked with cedar

Serves 4	750 g/1½ lb plain flour
	225 g/7½ oz coarse salt
Preparation time: 35 minutes	2 large eggs, lightly beaten
Cooking time: 20 minutes	32 grelot or other small onions, peeled
Ingredients:	1 piece of burnt cedar bark or cone
65 g/2½ oz butter, softened	1 small potato, about 25 g/1 oz
32 morel mushrooms	250 g/8 oz ground ivy
	2 egg yolks
	1 teaspoon Cognac
	1 teaspoon port
	50 ml/2 fl oz vegetable stock, optional (see page 184)
	fine salt and pepper

Method:

Melt 20 g/¾ oz of the butter, season with salt and pepper, then use to coat the morel mushrooms.

Sift the flour into a bowl and add the coarse salt. Rub in the remaining butter with your fingertips, then stir in the eggs and about 200 ml/7 fl oz water to make a smooth dough.

Divide the dough into 4 equal pieces and roll each piece into a round. Divide the morels and onions among the rounds and add a piece of cedar bark or cone to each. Fold the dough over to make a turnover, pinching the edges together firmly, and cook in a preheated oven, 220°C (425°F), Gas Mark 7, for 20–25 minutes. Prepare the sauce. Cook the potato in salted, boiling water for 15 minutes, then drain and mash into a purée. Pass the ground ivy through a juicer or process with a little water in a blender and then sieve the mixture.

Mix the ground ivy juice with thepotato, egg yolks, Cognac and port, season with salt and pepper, then heat gently. If the sauce is too thick, thin with a little vegetable stock. Invite your guests to break the salt crust before pouring the sauce over the mushrooms and onions.

Chef's tip Morels can be found in woodland clearings, wherever the soil is rich in nitrogen. Ground ivy (not to be confused with climbing ivy) resembles wild mangetouts. Its earthy flavour evokes moss and button mushrooms. You can use tarragon, sage or sorrel in its place.

Sunflower hearts with sweet vinaigrette, grated potato fritters and chanterelles with a lovage gazpacho

Serves 4

Preparation time: 50 minutes
Cooking time: 10 minutes

Ingredients:
4 sunflower hearts
4 large lovage sprigs
200 g/7 oz Swiss chard leaves (without ribs)
3 tablespoons breadcrumbs

3 tablespoons olive oil
2 tablespoons white wine vinegar
5 pinches of sugar
3 potatoes
2 eggs, beaten
1 tablespoon plain flour
3 tablespoons crème fraîche
1 litre/1¾ pints oil, for deep frying
475 g/15 oz small grey chanterelle mushrooms
6 parsley sprigs, chopped
fine salt, coarse salt, pepper

Method:

Cut off the sunflower stems, remove any leaves and cook the sunflower hearts in boiling water for 5–8 minutes, then refresh under cold water and drain. Reserve 4 lovage sprigs for garnish, pick the leaves from the remaining stalks and rinse well.

Blanch the chard leaves in boiling water for 1 minute, then drain.

Mix together the breadcrumbs, 100 ml/ 3½ fl oz water, 125 g/4 oz ice cubes, the lovage leaves, 2 tablespoons olive oil, 1 tablespoon vinegar and the chard in a bowl. Add a little salt and sugar to obtain a sweet-and-sour flavour, then chill the gazpacho in the refrigerator.

Grate the potatoes and mix with the beaten eggs, flour, crème fraîche, 2 pinches of sugar and some salt.

Heat the oil for deep-frying to 180–190°C/350–375°F or until a cube of bread browns in 30 seconds.

Mix the mushrooms with the parsley and remaining olive oil and vinegar. Season with salt and pepper.

Using a spoon, shape the potato mixture loosely into 4 balls and immerse in the hot oil. Deep-fry until golden.

Pour a little gazpacho on to each of 4 plates, in the shape of a tear. Arrange the mushrooms and sunflower hearts in a small mound, and place a potato fritter to the side. Garnish with a sprig of lovage and some coarse grains of salt, then serve immediately.

Chef's tip To avoid washing the mushrooms, which makes them absorb water and ruins their delicate flavour, scrape the stalks with a knife to remove any dirt or twigs. Lovage is a Mediterranean plant which was very popular in the past and is still used widely in salads and soups in Germany and England. The leaves taste of celery and concentrated stock. The roots can be dried and ground as a substitute for pepper. The cooked stems taste of angelica, and the spicy seeds are used to season pickled vegetables, marinades and fromage frais.

Asparagus flan with hazelnuts, quail's eggs and praline sauce

Serves 4

Preparation time: 1 hour

Cooking time: 15 minutes

Ingredients:

125 g/4 oz potatoes

145 g/4¾ oz egg whites, about 5 whites

140 g/4½ oz butter

100 g/3½ oz ground hazelnuts

100 g/3½ oz plain flour

1 large bunch of asparagus, peeled

15 g/½ oz crushed hazelnuts

200 ml/7 fl oz chicken stock (see page 184)

125 ml/4 fl oz white wine vinegar

100 ml/3½ fl oz white wine

200 ml/7 fl oz single cream

200 ml/7 fl oz milk

5 juniper berries

1 teaspoon praline paste

16 quail's eggs

salt

Method:

Cook the potatoes in salted, boiling water for 20 minutes, then drain and mash. Whisk the egg whites until they form peaks.

Melt 125 g/4 oz of the butter. Mix together the ground hazelnuts, flour, melted butter, mashed potatoes and salt. Gently fold in the egg whites.

Cook the asparagus in salted, boiling water until just tender, then refresh under cold water and drain. Separate the tips from the stems and arrange alternately in a buttered pie dish. Cover with the potato dough in a layer about 5 mm/¼ inch thick and bake in a preheated oven, 140°C (275°F), Gas Mark 1, for 20 minutes.

Roast the crushed hazelnuts in the oven or in a dry frying pan, then place in a saucepan with the stock, 100 ml/3½ fl oz of the vinegar, the wine, cream and milk. Bring to the boil and cook for 5 minutes. Blend with a hand-held blender and strain, then add the juniper and praline. Keep warm in a bain-marie.

Poach the eggs in simmering water with the remaining vinegar for 30 seconds. Refresh in iced water to stop any further cooking and drain on a cloth.

Cut the flan into 4 pieces and serve with the poached eggs and hazelnut sauce.

Chef's tip This can also be made in little individual flan dishes, in which case reduce the cooking time by 10 minutes. Avoid cooking at excessive temperatures as this will impair the colour. Hazelnuts complement the flavour of asparagus beautifully. It is important to strain the sauce in order to refine the texture and eliminate any flouriness caused by the ground hazelnuts.

Robert BLANC
DE JANVIER A JUILLET
ASPERGES VERTES
MARSEILLE PARIS LONDRES

Asparagus, the harbinger of spring

Star names
for this impressive asparagus.

All twisted and vibrant, little spikes appear all over the hillsides during the first days of spring. These fine, delicate stems are wild asparagus.

On the plains, it is a much more serious business. In Villelaure, père Blanc's asparagus is legendary. Some are as big as leeks. The most impressive variety is the 'brigitte', voluptuous like Brigitte Bardot, whereas the 'danielles' are tall like Danielle Darrieux and the 'mireilles' are petite like Mireille Mathieu. With the soul of a storyteller and the temperament of a farmer, père Blanc thinks of his asparagus as his daughters. He has devised a special method of packaging them in jars to protect the tips. His son Jean-Pierre has grown up among the asparagus and speaks with the dialect and passion of his father: 'Look how well the little ones are growing!' As he speaks, he treads delicately around a carefully packaged case destined for Norway, as if it contained bottles of fine wine. Another case is destined for Brussels, containing asparagus packed with the stems in water like delicate flowers. Some of the greatest chefs obtain their supplies of asparagus here. Yesterday, it was Chapel and Point. Today, Loiseau, Sammut, Pacaud, Senderens or, of course, Édouard Loubet. This asparagus is nourished by the rich alluvium deposited on the light soil of the Durance. Jean-Pierre slices the ends off the asparagus using a guillotine, then trims each one individually like a flower. He explains that the Provençal word for peeling is *plumer* (rather than the French *éplucher*). All this comes at a price. This asparagus costs 20 euros per kilo compared with only 6 euros per kilo for traditionally grown asparagus. But Édouard rates this asparagus alongside beef or lobster.

The asparagus
is graded and tied into bunches.

Goat's cheese and bread

Acidic one-day-old curd cheese with juniper honey • Ewe's milk yogurt with thyme flowers • Tomme made from Sivergues goat's milk and Chantebelle ewe's milk • Brousse from the du Castellas farm, with woodland aromas • Bourriol of burnt flour and bearded white spelt • Bread with cedar pine nuts, spruce and cypress from Florence

Acidic one-day-old curd cheese with juniper honey

For 1 litre/1¾ pints ewe's milk

Preparation time: 5 minutes

Cooking time: none

Ingredients:

500 g/1 lb curd cheese

4 tablespoons clear honey

8 juniper berries

Method:

Ladle the curd cheese into dishes. Using a spoon, make a hole in the middle of the curd cheese and fill with the honey and juniper berries.

Serve very cold, with plenty of crusty rustic bread.

Chef's tip Curd cheese is made during the first stage of cheese production, when hot milk is combined with rennet. Long ago, curd cheese and Brousse were the ordinary fare of peasants who would eat these cheeses at the end of a long hard day. One-day-old curd cheese can also be eaten as a dessert accompanied by redcurrants from the garden or a generous spoonful of strawberry jam.

Ewe's milk yogurt with thyme flowers

For 1 litre/1¾ pints ewe's milk

Preparation time: 15 minutes

Cooking time: 5 minutes

Standing time: 3 hours

Ingredients:

1 natural yogurt

4 teaspoons lemon juice

100 g/3½ oz sugar

3 drops of rennet

10 thyme flowers

Method:

Heat the milk to 27°C/81°F.

Mix together the yogurt, sugar, rennet and thyme flowers.

Pour the milk over the mixture and leave to stand at 27°C/81°F (in a bain-marie or at room temperature) for 3 hours.

Pour into pots. Cover with clingfilm.

Chef's tip You could use yogurt instead of the rennet. I adore the slightly acidic flavour of ewe's milk, but you can also use semi-skimmed cow's milk. Thyme flowers have a slight sweetness which enhances the flavour of the yogurt. Furthermore, thyme flowers immediately after the lambing season, when the milk is extraordinarily good. Why not serve these yogurts in little glass pots?

Tomme made from Sivergues goat's milk and Chantebelle ewe's milk

For 1 Tomme

Preparation time: 30 minutes
Cooking time: 15 minutes

Ingredients:

500 ml/17 fl oz goat's milk
500 ml/17 fl oz ewe's milk
a few drops of rennet
salt

Ricotta

Nothing is wasted in the mountains. After making Tomme cheese, the whey remaining in the vat is heated to boiling point. The cream which rises to the surface is collected. Once cooled, the remaining whey is fed to the pigs.

La caillette (ancestral cheese)

The stomachs of lambs or kids are emptied and cleaned, collecting the gastric juices which are then used to curdle fresh milk. The stomachs are filled with the curds and matured in the cellar where a fire is lit to give them a slight smoked flavour.

Method:

Heat the milk to 35°C/95°F. Add the rennet and leave to curdle.

Stir to separate the curds from the whey. Mould the curds into a cheese strainer and leave to drain.

Sprinkle both surfaces of the cheese with salt. Cover with a weight to facilitate drainage and give the cheese a compact texture. Wait until firm before eating.

Ewe's milk Tomme, also known as Tomme du Roucas

Just after milking, rennet is added to the milk. One hour later, the milk is stirred over a low heat. The curds are then drained and placed into moulds. Next day, the fresh Tomme is rubbed with salt and stored in the cellar to mature.

As the milk is poured into the vat, I can smell all the aromas of the mountain: oak leaf, thyme, savory and clover. Adding salt seems to 'fix' these aromas and brings out their flavours on the palate.

Opposite:
David Ladu prepares the curds which will be used to make Tomme cheese.

Chef's tip Ideally, the cheese should be pressed on a plank of spruce, an aromatic wood low in tannin (compared with oak, for example).

Brousse from the du Castellas farm, with woodland aromas

Serves 4

Preparation time: 15 minutes
Cooking time: 40 minutes

Ingredients:

4 maincrop Pertuis potatoes or other
baking potatoes, unpeeled
1 lettuce

2 tablespoons vinegar
1 garlic clove, finely chopped
4 tablespoons olive oil
a few pistils of wild flowers,
such as rocket or spring onion
1 Brousse
4 slices of smoked country ham
8 slices of dry smoked sausage
salt and pepper

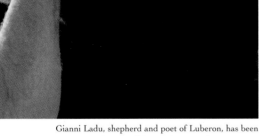

Gianni Ladu, shepherd and poet of Luberon, has been
supplying cheese to Édouard for more than ten years.

Method:

Sprinkle the potatoes with salt and then wrap in foil. Cook in embers or in a preheated oven, 200°C (400°F), Gas Mark 6, for about 40 minutes. The cooking time will vary depending on their size. Turn at the end of 30 minutes. Separate the lettuce leaves. Mix together the vinegar, garlic, oil, salt and pepper to make a vinaigrette.

Toss the lettuce in the vinaigrette just before serving.

Add the pistils of wild flowers.

Place the Brousse on a dish and grill until lightly coloured. Serve accompanied by the potatoes, salad, ham and sausage.

Chef's tip Pertuis is a neighbouring village famous for its potatoes. To prepare Brousse yourself, gently heat 1 litre/ 1¾ pints milk to 92°C/198°F (but do not boil), skimming the surface with a ladle. Pour into a cheese strainer and leave to drain for a few hours. In Provence, we like our Brousse quite dry, crumbly and grainy, made with skimmed milk, and we eat it on its own with just olive oil and some coarse salt. In the past, farmers would drink the whey resulting from the production of Tomme and Brousse, but nowadays it is given to the pigs. This low-fat liquid is really just milky water with a sourish flavour. I use it a lot in my cooking, especially for marinating fish or as a base for sauces.

Bourriol of burnt flour
and bearded white spelt

Makes about 1.2 kg/2½ lb loaf

Preparation time: 30 minutes
Standing time: 45 minutes
Cooking time: 35 minutes

Ingredients:

25 g/1 oz salt

400 g/13 oz boiled potatoes, mashed

40 g/1½ oz fresh yeast

100 ml/3½ fl oz lukewarm milk

400 g/13 oz cooked spelt

200 g/7 oz spelt flour

5 eggs

50 g/2 oz lightly smoked streaky bacon
or pork belly, diced

Method:
Add the salt to the mashed potatoes. Dissolve the yeast in the warmed milk.

Mix the mashed potatoes with the yeast, then stir in the cooked spelt, flour, eggs and bacon or pork belly. If necessary, add a little water to produce a smooth dough. Leave the dough to rise in a warm place for 45 minutes, before sliding it into a nonstick frying pan.

Cook over a low heat for 30 minutes, then cover the pan with foil and cook for a further 5 minutes.

Chef's tip The recipe for this bread goes back to the time before modern ovens, when women would leave the dough to rise in the pan. A crust would form through contact with the air. It would be cooked over a low heat, either just cooked on one side and covered at the end of cooking, or turned half way through cooking. Provence is very keen on spelt, an ancient grain revived on the harsh clay soil in the land of olive trees. Less suitable for making bread than wheat, spelt had previously been forgotten. The cooked grains of spelt burst in the mouth when you bite into this bread. I like to eat this bread warm, drizzled with olive oil and garnished with a steamed potato. I eat it every morning in the kitchen with a spoonful of mashed potatoes. In spring, it is delicious with raw broad beans and peas dressed with vinaigrette, restored to its rightful position at the centre of a meal. This bread can also be cooked individually, like blinis.

Bread with cedar pine nuts, spruce and cypress from Florence

Makes 1 kg/2 lb loaf or 10 rolls

Preparation time: 30 minutes
Standing time: 45 minutes
Cooking time: 15 minutes

Ingredients:

35 g/1¼ oz fresh yeast

500 g/1 lb plain flour, plus extra
for dusting

75 g/3 oz multigrain flour

75 g/3 oz wholemeal flour

400 ml/14 fl oz water

15 g/½ oz salt

200 g/7 oz cedar pine nuts

50 g/2 oz pine or spruce buds

20 g/¾ oz fresh cypress shoots

1 egg, for glazing

Method:
Dissolve the yeast in a little lukewarm water. Knead all the flours with the yeast, cold water and salt, making sure that the salt does not come into contact with the yeast.

Finally, mix in the pine nuts, pine or spruce buds and cypress shoots, then leave to rise in a warm place for 45 minutes.

Knead the dough again. Divide the dough into 10 portions and roll each one into a ball. Place these balls on a baking sheet, glaze with the beaten egg and dust with flour.

Cook in a preheated oven, 240°C (475°F), Gas Mark 9, for about 5 minutes, until the rolls are golden, then lower the temperature to 200°C (400°F), Gas Mark 6 and cook for a further 8–10 minutes.

Chef's tip If you want to make one or two large loaves rather than individual rolls, cook in a preheated oven, 240°C (475°F), Gas Mark 9 for 15 minutes, then at 200°C (400°F), Gas Mark 6 for 10 minutes.

The lambing season and the first milking of spring

In the hills, home to Gianni – Édouard's goatherd – sheep and goats spend the warm nights under the stars, dotted along the upper slopes, feeding on acorns and undergrowth. In the early hours, they return to the sheepfold for milking; they then spend the afternoon in the cool under the trees. On smallholdings of between sixty and one hundred animals, like Gianni's, milking is still carried out entirely by hand.

In late autumn three or four male goats approach the flock, though in fact only the eldest will mate. When the time comes, the others keep their distance – being younger they give way to the most senior among them. An essential strategy this, given that one billy-goat requires between forty and fifty females to satisfy him!

In spring, from March to April, after a pregnancy of five and a half months, the sheep and goats give birth. The rich milk, which they produce at this time, is reserved for the lambs and kids, who eagerly suck on their mothers' teats. They remain in the sheep pen for a month or so while their mothers, on the other hand, freely come and go between feeds; with all this activity and exertion they continue gambolling in the hills in search of fresh shoots and foliage – albeit at a somewhat gentler pace.

At Easter, around a third of the lambs are taken away for slaughter, while the others will remain to renew the flock. With the lambing season over, the production of goat's and ewe's milk cheese resumes and will continue until the next cycle begins in November.

At home, Gianni certainly knows how to welcome his guests: warm *bugne de Brousse fraîche* (little puffs of a whey *fromage blanc* in a very light batter), best eaten with a sprig of mint, *Brousse*, *caillette* (a stunning cheese, first smoked then dried – smooth as butter yet quite strong and sharp), roast lamb with a creamy texture...Nearby Gianni's son, David (incidentally, one of the children who danced in the famous clip from *La Lambada*) makes his own *caillé* and *Brousse*, as well as a delicious Tomme which Édouard serves at his restaurant.

Left:
Ingrid and Gianni
du Castellas,
with Antonio (centre).

Opposite above:
The Roucas farm
at Chantebelle.

Middle:
After lambing,
cheese-making resumes.

Opposite below:
Gianni's herd of goats
walking along a high pass.

Desserts

Iced soup of bitter chocolate, floating islands of yarrow meringue and ice cream with garden tansy • Cherry jam with vervain and Sichuan pepper • Three crème brûlées with a hint of springtime • Onion confit with green pepper, red côtes-du-Luberon and violets • Acacia fritters and ice cream with woodruff • Couturas cherries and blancmange made with cream and Lourmarin almond milk, flavoured with cherry kernels • Cherry clafoutis with financier sponge, based on my grandmother Raymonde's recipe • Granita of lemon, or limoncello, with coriander leaves and seeds • Lacy tuiles and green aniseed, with red wine granita • Mimosa eggs and wheat grass juice, with angelica ice cream • My grandmother's floating islands with milk 'jam' and scorpion broom • Sunburst of red berries sautéed with sugar, red wine and sage, served with ice cream made from my goatherd's Brousse • Millefeuille of raspberries, Chiboust with cardamom and cloud of pistachio • Baba, named after Ali Baba of *One Thousand and One Nights*, steeped in rum with pinks

Iced soup of bitter chocolate, floating islands of yarrow meringue and ice cream with garden tansy

Serves 4

Preparation time: 20 minutes

Cooking time: 10 minutes

Freezing time: 45 minutes

Ingredients:

125 g/4 oz dark chocolate

135 g/4½ oz caster sugar

15 g/½ oz cocoa powder

125 ml/4 fl oz espresso coffee

500 ml/17 fl oz milk

5 egg yolks

2 egg whites

50 g/2 oz yarrow, plus extra to decorate

100 ml/3½ fl oz génépi liqueur

Method:

Combine the chocolate, 40 g/1½ oz of the sugar, the cocoa, coffee and 400 ml/ 14 fl oz water in a saucepan. Bring to the boil, remove from the heat and leave to cool.

Gently heat 100 ml/3½ fl oz of the milk until warm, then mix with the egg yolks and 50 g/2 oz of the remaining sugar. Bring the remaining milk to a rolling boil and immediately pour on to the egg yolk mixture, stirring constantly. Return to the pan and heat, stirring constantly, for 2–3 minutes, until thickened and the mixture coats the back of the spoon. Strain over the yarrow and leave to infuse for 7 minutes. Remove and discard the yarrow. Leave the mixture to cool, then freeze in an ice cream maker.

Whisk the egg whites until they form peaks, then whisk in the remaining sugar and the génépi.

Shape the mixture into 8 mounds on a microwave-proof dish and cook in a microwave on medium power for 30 seconds. Leave to cool.

Just before serving, drop a few ice cubes into the chocolate soup. Pour into bowls. Add 2 scoops of ice cream to each and crown with the meringue floating islands. Decorate with yarrow sprigs.

Chef's tip I use an ice cream scoop to shape my floating islands. I regularly use coffee in my cooking and pastries. Its bitter flavour enhances the flavours of the other ingredients. Instead of the yarrow in the ice cream, you could use another aromatic herb or spice which goes well with the génépi, such as exotic mint or aniseed.

Cherry jam with vervain and Sichuan pepper

Makes 4 kg/8¾ lb

Preparation time: 40 minutes

Maceration time: 12 hours

Cooking time: 30 minutes

Ingredients:

3 kg/6½ lb cherries

2.1 kg/4 lb 9 oz sugar

3 vervain sprigs

25 g/1 oz Sichuan pepper

Method:

Pit the cherries, reserving the stones in a square of muslin. Place the cherries in a dish with the sugar and vervain, and leave to macerate in the refrigerator for 12 hours.

Grind and sift the Sichuan pepper.

Place the cherries in a preserving pan, bring to the boil and boil for 2 minutes. Remove half the cherries and set aside. Add the muslin square to the pan and boil for a further 10 minutes.

Remove and discard the muslin bag and process the cherries in a food processor or blender.

Pour the purée back into the pan with the reserved cherries and Sichuan pepper. Bring to the boil, stirring to prevent the mixture from scorching on the base of the pan. Ladle into jars sterilized with boiling water, screw on the lids immediately, turn the jars upside down and leave to cool.

Chef's tip I process the cherries because I don't like jam which is too chunky, but I purée only half of them because I don't like jam which is too smooth either. In my opinion, this produces the perfect texture. I enjoy this jam on Breton shortbread. The flavours of the fruit and the butter explode on the tastebuds. A perfect snack at any time of the day.

Three crème brûlées
with a hint of springtime

Serves 8–9

Preparation time: 45 minutes
Cooking time: 50 minutes
Chilling time: 16 hours

Cherry crème brûlée:
6 egg yolks
40 g/1½ oz brown sugar
175 ml/6 fl oz milk
500 ml/17 fl oz single cream
150 g/5 oz pitted cherries

Acacia crème brûlée:
5 egg yolks
50 g/2 oz brown sugar
175 ml/6 fl oz milk
500 ml/17 fl oz single cream
25 g/1 oz acacia flowers

Philodendron crème brûlée:
5 egg yolks
65 g/2½ oz brown sugar
175 ml/6 fl oz milk
500 ml/17 fl oz single cream
15 g/½ oz philodendron leaves

Method:

Cherry crème brûlée:

Whisk the egg yolks with the sugar until thickened and smooth. Add the milk and half the cream. Bring the remaining cream to simmering point, pour over the cherries and leave to infuse for 8 minutes. Strain, stir into the egg yolk mixture, cover and chill in the refrigerator overnight.

Pour the mixture into ramekins and bake in a preheated oven, 90°C (190°F), Gas Low, for 45 minutes. Cool and chill in the refrigerator for at least 6 hours. Before serving, caramelize with a salamander, or culinary blow torch or place briefly under a preheated grill.

Acacia crème brûlée:

Whisk the egg yolks with the sugar until thickened and smooth. Add the milk and half the cream. Bring the remaining cream to simmering point, pour over the acacia flowers and leave to infuse for 8 minutes. Strain, stir into the egg yolk mixture, cover and chill in the refrigerator overnight.

Pour the mixture into ramekins and bake in a preheated oven, 90°C (190°F), Gas Low, for 45 minutes. Cool and chill in the refrigerator for at least 6 hours. Before serving, caramelize with a salamander or culinary blow torch or place briefly under a preheated grill.

Philodendron crème brûlée:

Whisk the egg yolks with the sugar until thickened and smooth. Add the milk and half the cream. Bring the remaining cream to simmering point, pour over the philodendron leaves and leave to infuse for 8 minutes. Strain, stir into the egg yolk mixture, cover and chill in the refrigerator overnight.

Pour the mixture into ramekins and bake in a preheated oven, 90°C (190°F), Gas Low, for 45 minutes. Cool and chill in the refrigerator for at least 6 hours. Before serving, caramelize with a salamander or culinary blow torch or place briefly under a preheated grill.

Chef's tip At the restaurant, I serve these crème brûlées in miniature soup tureens so that I can offer several flavours. As well as cherry, acacia and philodendron, I also offer crème brûlées flavoured with pine cone, lavender and rum.

Onion confit with green pepper, red côtes-du-Luberon and violets

Serves 4

Preparation time: 15 minutes

Cooking time: 1½ hours

Ingredients:

4 large white onions, peeled

250 ml/8 fl oz white wine

600 g/1 lb 5 oz sugar

1 unsprayed lemon, quartered

3 vanilla pods, split open and scraped

1 cinnamon stick

20 g/¾ oz green peppercorns

1 piece of orange rind (unsprayed)

1 bottle of red côtes-du-Luberon wine

1 teaspoon cornflour

2 generous handfuls of violet flowers

Method:

Place the onions in a large saucepan with the white wine, 400 g/13 oz of the sugar, the lemon quarters, vanilla pods, cinnamon, half the peppercorns and the orange rind. Poach for 1½ hours, until extremely soft. Remove from the heat, cool and chill in the refrigerator.

Pour the red wine into a saucepan with the remaining sugar and peppercorns. Bring to the boil, then lower the heat and simmer for about 20 minutes, until reduced by one-quarter.

Mix the cornflour with a little water, stir into the pan and cook for 2 minutes, until thickened. Strain, cool and reserve in the refrigerator.

Arrange 1 onion on each of 4 plates. Drizzle with the sauce and sprinkle with violet flowers before serving.

Chef's tip This dessert should be decorated lavishly with violet flowers. The violets should not be cooked as this impairs their delicate flavour. Only dried violets tolerate heat. If you cannot get hold of fresh violets, infuse 7 g/⅜ oz dried violets and 3 g/⅛ oz dried jasmine in the juice.

Acacia fritters and ice cream with woodruff

Serves 4

Preparation time: 30 minutes

Cooking time: 10 minutes

Freezing time: 45 minutes

Ingredients:

1 litre/1¾ pints milk

10 egg yolks

200 g/7 oz granulated sugar

15 g/½ oz woodruff flowers
(available from herbalists)

2 litres/3½ pints oil, for deep-frying

2 handfuls of acacia flowers,
plus 4 sprigs for decoration

25 g/1 oz icing sugar

Tempura batter:

3 tablespoons plain flour

1 tablespoon cornflour

4 tablespoons water

Method:

Heat 200 ml/7 fl oz of the milk until warm. Meanwhile, whisk the egg yolks with the granulated sugar. Whisk in the warm milk.

Bring the remaining milk to the boil, then pour on to the egg yolks all at once, return to the pan and heat for 1 minute. Place the woodruff flowers in a bowl, pour the custard over them and leave to infuse for 15 minutes. Strain and freeze in an ice cream maker.

Heat the oil for deep-frying to 180–190°C/350–375°F or until a cube of bread browns in 30 seconds. Meanwhile, make the tempura batter by mixing all the ingredients with 6 ice cubes. Dip the acacia flowers into this batter. Lower spoonfuls of the coated flowers into the hot oil, turning rapidly before they colour. Drain on kitchen paper and sprinkle with icing sugar.

Arrange scoops of ice cream and the fritters on 4 plates. Decorate with acacia sprigs and serve.

Chef's tip Woodruff has a sweetish flavour similar to vanilla, coconut and fig tree blossom, all of which can be substituted for woodruff (boil coconut in milk first). Woodruff also has aromas of the vanilla-scented wild orchid, a rare and protected plant, and a sweet taste of pollen reminiscent of acacia. If I need a softer batter, I replace the tempura batter with a mixture of choux pastry slackened with milk. These fritters can also be cooked like popcorn, in a frying pan with a little oil, and assembled in a millefeuille arrangement with the ice cream.

Couturas cherries and blancmange made with cream and Lourmarin almond milk, flavoured with cherry kernels

Serves 4

Preparation time: 20 minutes

Cooking time: 15 minutes

Ingredients:

2 leaves of gelatine

25 g/1 oz whole shelled almonds

150 ml/¼ pint milk

125 g/4 oz caster sugar

150 ml/¼ pint single cream

350 g/11½ oz cherries (pigeon's heart, bigarreau or Napoleon)

4 tablespoons lemon juice

1 angelica sprig

Method:

Place the gelatine in a small bowl of cold water and set aside to soften. Place the almonds and milk in a saucepan and bring to the boil. Drain, reserving the milk. Wrap the almonds in a tea towel and rub between your fingers to slide off the skins. Return the milk to pan, bring back to the boil, then process with the almonds. Transfer to a bowl. Drain the gelatine and add to the milk mixture with 50 g/2 oz of sugar. Stir well, then leave to cool. Beat the cream and combine with the cooled almond mixture. Divide among 4 small dishes or moulds.

Reserve about 20 cherries. Place the remainder in a high-sided frying pan with the lemon juice, 25 ml/1 fl oz water, the remaining sugar and the angelica. Bring to the boil over a low heat. Crush the mixture and sieve.

Steam the reserved cherries for 20 seconds, then remove from the heat.

Turn out the blancmange on to individual serving plates, drizzle with the cherry juice and sprinkle with cherries.

Chef's tip The jellified cherry juice has a slightly sour aftertaste which contrasts with the almonds. Angelica imparts a fresh 'green' flavour to the cherry juice.

Cherry clafoutis with financier sponge, based on my grandmother Raymonde's recipe

Serves 4

Preparation time: 20 minutes
Cooking time: 25 minutes

Ingredients:
575 ml/18 fl oz milk
4 eggs
125 g/4 oz sugar
50g/2 oz plain flour
pinch of salt
125 g/4 oz butter, softened
100 g/3½ oz ground almonds
250 g/8 oz cherries

Method:

Heat the milk until warm. Meanwhile, whisk 2 eggs with 2 teaspoons of the sugar. Add 6 tablespoons of the flour, the salt and the warm milk.

Cream 100 g/3½ oz of butter, then beat in 100 g/3½ oz of the remaining sugar, the rest of the flour, the almonds and the remaining eggs. Combine the mixtures. Butter the dish and dust with sugar.

Arrange the cherries in the base of the dish and pour over batter. Bake in a preheated oven, 160°C (325°F), Gas Mark 3, for 20 minutes.
Serve warm or cold.

Chef's tip I inherited this recipe from my grandmother Raymonde. She uses whole cherries, with their stalks intact, and plants them in the batter with the stalks in the air. I have continued this tradition. As it emerges from the oven, the golden clafoutis gives off aromas of almond and cherry stone, bristling with cherry stalks sticking out of the batter.

Granita of lemon, or limoncello, with coriander leaves and seeds

Serves 4

Preparation time: 20 minutes
Cooking time: 5 minutes
Freezing time: 45 minutes

Ingredients:
rind of ½ lemon
30 g/1¼ oz glucose
160 g/5¼ oz sugar
325 ml/11 fl oz lemon juice
1 teaspoon coriander seeds
4 coriander leaves

Method:

Bring 450 ml/¾ pint water to the boil with the lemon rind, glucose and sugar.

Strain, add the lemon juice and set aside to cool.
When cold, freeze in an ice cream maker.

Sprinkle with coriander seeds and leaves before serving.

Chef's tip If you do not have an ice cream maker, pour the mixture into a shallow dish and place in the freezer for 30 minutes. Scrape off the ice crystals forming at the edge of the dish, stir well and return to the freezer. Repeat this process until the granita is completely frozen.

Lacy tuiles and green aniseed, with red wine granita

Serves 4

Preparation time: 35 minutes
Cooking time: 15 minutes
Freezing time: 45 minutes

Tuiles:

40 g/1½ oz butter, melted

100 g/3½ oz sugar

25 g/1 oz plain flour

1½ teaspoons pastis

2 teaspoons green aniseed

oil, for greasing

Granita:

500 ml/17 fl oz red wine

100 g/3½ oz sugar

2 teaspoons glucose

10 juniper berries

1 angelica leaf

Method:

To make the granita, bring the wine to the boil with 5 tablespoons water, the sugar, glucose and 5 juniper berries. Crush the remaining juniper berries with a knife, place in a bowl with the angelica and pour over the wine mixture. Leave to infuse for 7 minutes. Strain, cool, then pour into an ice cream maker.

To make the tuiles, cream the melted butter with the sugar. Stir in the flour, then the pastis, 2 tablespoons water and the aniseed. Lightly oil a baking sheet and place spoonfuls of the mixture on it, spaced well apart. Bake in a preheated oven, 180°C (350°F), Gas Mark 4, for 3–4 minutes.

To serve, place scoops of the granita in individual dishes and crown with tuiles.

Chef's tip For this granita, I use a Syrah known as Lafond-du-broc. At the restaurant, I make long rectangular tuiles shaped like matchsticks, creating handy bite-size delicacies.

Mimosa eggs and wheat grass juice, with angelica ice cream

Serves 4

Preparation time: 25 minutes
Cooking time: 25 minutes
Chilling and freezing time: 4 hours

Ingredients:

400 ml/14 fl oz single cream
1 tablespoon mimosa flowers
750 g/1½ lb white chocolate, chopped
450 g/14½ oz cocoa butter
1 pineapple, peeled, cored and chopped
1 generous handful of wheat grass
150 ml/¼ pint lemon juice
125 g/4 oz sugar
1 thyme sprig
1 small rosemary sprig
1 litre/1¾ pints milk
10 egg yolks
250 ml/8 fl oz crème fraîche
1 generous handful of angelica leaves

Method:

To prepare the mimosa eggs, heat 200 ml/ 7 fl oz of single cream and infuse with the mimosa. Bring to the boil, then pour over 200 g/7 oz of chopped white chocolate. Chill in the refrigerator.

Beat the remaining single cream, then beat it into the chilled mixture until thick and combined.

Next, prepare the chocolate coating. Melt the remaining white chocolate with the cocoa butter in a heatproof bowl set over a pan of simmering water, stir and keep warm.

Process the pineapple, wheat grass, lemon juice and 2 tablespoons of sugar, in a food processor or blender, then strain into a bowl. Add the thyme and rosemary and leave to infuse.

Bring the milk to the boil over a high heat. Whisk the egg yolks with the remaining sugar. Whisk in a little of the hot milk, then pour the mixture into the saucepan of milk and cook, stirring constantly, for 3 minutes, or until the

custard coats the back of the spoon. Pour over the angelica, process with a hand-held blender and strain. Stir in the crème fraîche and pour into an ice cream maker. Fill 8 semi-spherical moulds with the mimosa egg mixture and place in the freezer for at least 2 hours. Remove the mimosa half-eggs from the moulds once they have frozen.

Assemble 2 half-eggs to form a whole one. Dip the egg twice in the warm chocolate coating and place in the refrigerator for 45 minutes. Repeat with the remaining half-eggs and chocolate coating. Serve with the wheat grass juice and angelica ice cream.

Chef's tip I adore fresh angelica. Everyone has tasted candied angelica stems, but the leaves are rarely used. Nutritionally speaking, they are particularly appropriate in desserts because they promote digestion. If you do not have any semi-spherical moulds, use little ramekins.

My grandmother's floating islands with milk 'jam' and scorpion broom

Serves 4

Preparation time: 30 minutes

Cooking time: 1 hour

Ingredients:

2 litres/3½ pints milk

150 g/5 oz scorpion broom, plus broom flowers to decorate

350 g/11½ oz sugar

1 vanilla pod

1 leaf of gelatine

1 teaspoon bicarbonate of soda

3 egg whites

Method:

Gently heat 1 litre/1¾ pints of the milk, skimming off and reserving the skin as it forms on the surface.

Mamie Loubet, a cordon bleu cook, guided Edward's first steps in the kitchen.

Add the broom to the remaining milk, leave to infuse, then strain. Pour the infused milk into a saucepan, add 300 g/ 10 oz of the sugar and the vanilla and heat until reduced by half. Meanwhile soak the gelatine in a small bowl of water until softened, then drain. Remove the pan of milk from the heat and stir in the bicarbonate of soda and gelatine.

Whisk the egg whites in a grease-free bowl until they form peaks, then whisk in the remaining sugar. Shape the mixture into 8 small mounds on a dish and cook in a microwave on medium power for 20–30 seconds. Leave to cool.

Divide the milk jam, milk skin and floating islands among 4 dishes. Sprinkle with broom flowers and serve chilled.

Chef's tip In the past, milk could not be kept for as long as it is today. I have inherited this recipe from my grandmother who, like other women of her generation, used any leftover milk to make milk skin. She also used it to make fabulous cakes.

Sunburst of red berries sautéed with sugar, red wine and sage, served with ice cream made from my goatherd's Brousse

Serves 4

Preparation time: 35 minutes

Cooking time: 15 minutes

Freezing time: 45 minutes

Ingredients:

500 g/1 lb Brousse or other curd cheese

250 ml/8 fl oz single cream

500 ml/17 fl oz milk

3 egg yolks

230 g/7½ oz sugar

1 strip of lemon rind

400 g/13 oz mixed red berries

25 g/1 oz butter

8 sage leaves

50 ml/2 fl oz red wine, plus extra for drizzling

Method:

Beat the cheese with the cream until smooth, then set aside.

Heat 100 ml/3½ fl oz of the milk until warm. Whisk the egg yolks with 200 g/ 7 oz of the sugar, then stir in the warm milk. Bring the remaining milk to the boil over a high heat and pour it on to the egg yolk mixture all at once.

Add the lemon rind and return the mixture to the saucepan. Cook, stirring constantly, for 3 minutes, until the custard coats the back of the spoon.

Strain and leave to cool. Process with a hand-held blender, then place in an ice cream maker.

Place the berries in a pan with the remaining sugar and the butter and cook over a low heat. Add the sage leaves and deglaze with the red wine.

Divide the berries and scoops of ice cream among 4 plates. Drizzle with a few drops of wine before serving.

Chef's tip I cannot resist the pleasure of fresh berries in spring and summer: raspberries, strawberries, blueberries, blackberries, blackcurrants. This dessert is really a hot jam, where the fruit is cooked rapidly to preserve the flavour and texture.

Millefeuille of raspberries, Chiboust cream with cardamom and cloud of pistachio

Serves 4

Preparation time: 1½ hours
Cooking time: 20 minutes

Ingredients:
250 g/8 oz puff pastry
5 tablespoons icing sugar
1½ gelatine leaves
200 ml/7 fl oz milk

5 egg yolks, plus 1 egg white
175 g/6 oz granulated sugar
40 g/1½ oz plain flour
pinch of ground cardamom
300 ml/½ pint single cream
2 tablespoons pistachio paste
100 g/3½ oz rhubarb
100 ml/3½ fl oz lemon juice
2 punnets of wild strawberries
2 punnets of raspberries

Method:

Roll out the puff pastry very thinly and cut out 3 rounds. Place on a baking sheet and cover with another baking sheet to prevent the pastry from rising. Bake in a preheated oven, 200°C (400°F), Gas Mark 6, for 5 minutes. Remove the top baking sheet, dust the pastry rounds with icing sugar and bake for a few minutes more, until golden.

To make the Chiboust cream:

Soak the gelatine in a small bowl of cold water until softened. Bring the milk to the boil. Meanwhile, whisk the egg yolks with 20 g/¾ oz of granulated sugar and the flour. Add the cardamom. Pour on the boiling milk, stirring constantly, and return to the saucepan. Cook over a medium heat, stirring constantly, for about 4 minutes, until thick and smooth. Reserve one-third of the Chiboust cream. Drain the gelatine. Combine the remaining Chiboust cream with the gelatine, cover with clingfilm and leave to cool.

Whisk the egg white in a grease-free bowl until stiff. Heat 125 g/4 oz of the remaining granulated sugar over a low heat until it reaches 121°C/250°F (this will take about 5 minutes). If you do not have a sugar thermometer, test by dropping some of the cooked sugar into cold water; it should be possible to roll the sugar between your fingers into a soft ball. Pour this hot sugar over the egg white and whisk until completely cool. Beat the cream. Mix one-sixth of the cream with the pistachio paste and the reserved Chiboust cream.

Mix the remaining Chiboust cream with the meringue and remaining cream.

Cook the rhubarb with the lemon juice, the remaining granulated sugar and 100 ml/3½ fl oz water. Process with a hand-held blender and sieve. Using a piping bag, coat 1 pastry round with Chiboust cream to a depth of 1.5 cm/¾ inch and cover with wild strawberries. Arrange the raspberries in a circle on the 2 remaining puff pastry rounds, leaving a space at the centre. Fill the centre with the cardamom cream. Warm in the oven at a low temperature. Place 1 round on top of the other on a serving dish. Top with the pastry round coated with Chiboust cream. Serve immediately with the rhubarb sauce and Chiboust cream and pistachio mousse.

Chef's tip This recipe is for special occasions, suitable for a table of gourmets. Pistachio paste is available from pâtisserie wholesalers and in some Middle Eastern groceries. It can also be ordered from some pâtissiers. If you cannot get hold of pistachio paste, buy some dark green unsalted pistachios and grind finely with sugar.

Baba, named after Ali Baba of *One Thousand and One Nights*, steeped in rum with pinks

Serves 4

Preparation time: 35 minutes
Cooking time: 25 minutes
Standing time: 2–3 days
Steeping time: 1 hour

Ingredients:
100 ml/3½ fl oz lukewarm milk
15 g/½ oz fresh yeast

2 eggs
125 g/4 oz caster sugar
250 g/8 oz plain flour
pinch of salt
50 g/2 oz butter
oil, for greasing
125 ml/4 fl oz rum
10 pinks with stems
1 strip of lemon rind
1 clove
1 star anise
50 ml/2 fl oz marc brandy
1 small punnet of white currants, to decorate

Method:

First, make the dough. Mix together the milk and yeast in a small bowl. Beat the eggs with 2 teaspoons of the sugar with an electric mixer. Add the yeast and milk mixture, followed by the flour and salt. Mix for 5 minutes. Heat the butter until golden brown, then pour the hot butter into the dough.

Continue to mix for a further 5 minutes. Pour into a lightly oiled baba mould (only quarter-fill the mould as the dough will rise immediately). Cover with a tea towel and leave to stand at room temperature until the dough fills the mould. The crust should be smooth, shiny and pierced with tiny holes. Bake the baba in a preheated oven, 160°C (325°F), Gas Mark 3, for 20 minutes. Turn out of the mould. Leave to dry for 2–3 days.

To prepare the syrup, bring 1 litre/ 1¾ pints water to the boil, with the rum, remaining sugar, lemon rind, clove, star anise and pink stems (reserve the leaves and flowers). Leave to infuse for 10 minutes, then strain.

Dip the top of the baba in the syrup and leave to soak. Turn it over and dip the other side (which will soak up the syrup more quickly). Place on a rack and chill in the refrigerator for about 1 hour so that the sugar sets.

Blend the pink flowers with the marc brandy and coat the top of the baba with this sauce. Decorate with pink leaves and white currants.

Chef's tip I cook this dessert in May, when pinks are in flower. I created this recipe as a tribute to Jean Mignard, native of Aix-en-Provence who gave his name to the pink (known as *oeillet mignardise* in French). The baba was created by Stanislas Leszczynski who, during his exile in Poland, came upon the idea of dipping a kugelhopf in rum. He named his invention after his favourite hero, Ali Baba. Yet another illustration that cookery knows no boundaries.

Vinegars

Wormwood vinegar • Vinegar with thyme flowers • Fennel vinegar with cherry stalks

Wormwood vinegar

For 1 litre/1¾ pints cider vinegar

Preparation time: 5 minutes
Cooking time: 5 minutes
Infusion time: 2 days

Ingredients:
100 ml/3½ fl oz water
25 g/1 oz sugar
75 g/3 oz wormwood
1 wormwood sprig, to garnish

Method:
Bring the water to the boil with the sugar, then pour over the wormwood and leave to infuse for 6 minutes. Mix with the vinegar and leave to infuse on a sunny windowsill for 2 days. Strain and bottle, with a sprig of absinthe for garnish.

Vinegar with thyme flowers

For 1 litre/1¾ pints cider vinegar
Preparation time: 5 minutes
Cooking: time 5 minutes
Infusion time: 2 days

Ingredients:
100 ml/3½ fl oz water
25 g/1 oz sugar
50 g/2 oz thyme
1 thyme sprig, to garnish

Method:
Bring the water to the boil with the sugar, then pour over the thyme and leave to infuse for 6 minutes. Mix with the vinegar and leave to infuse on a sunny windowsill for 2 days.
Strain and bottle, with a sprig of thyme for garnish.

Fennel vinegar with cherry stalks

For 1 litre/1¾ pints white wine vinegar

Preparation time: 5 minutes
Cooking time: 5 minutes
Infusion time: 2 days

Ingredients:

100 ml/3½ fl oz water
25 g/1 oz sugar
50 g/2 oz cherry stalks
7 fennel sprigs
100 ml/3½ fl oz cherry juice

Method:

Bring the water to the boil with the sugar, then pour over the cherry stalks, reserving a few for garnish, and 6 sprigs of fennel.

Leave to infuse for 6 minutes, Mix with the vinegar and cherry juice and leave to infuse on a sunny windowsill for 2 days. Strain and bottle, with a sprig of fennel and cherry stalks for garnish.

Chef's tip

Natural vinegar, especially cider vinegar, is a universal remedy as well as a precious condiment. Rich in essential amino acids and enzymes, it is an astonishing reserve of vitamins and mineral salts, beneficial for many human diseases. A natural antiseptic, vinegar aids digestion, improves vitality and even prolongs youth. 'An apple a day keeps the doctor away', so the saying goes. Apply this principle by consuming the juice of an apple with some cider vinegar.

You can make mint vinegar by filling a bottle with fresh mint and then covering with hot vinegar. Cork and leave to stand for 4 weeks. Strain and use with vegetables, meats and cool drinks.

Aperitifs and infusions

Infusion of cherry stalks and roasted acorns • Angelica infusion • Kir with truffle wine and Luberon honey • Infusion of rose and lilac • Infusion of lovage • Spring kir with almond juice • Pastis with Luberon honey

Infusion of cherry stalks
and roasted acorns

For 1 litre/1¾ pints water

Preparation time: 5 minutes
Cooking time: 20 minutes
Infusion time: 7 minutes

Ingredients:

6 acorns

6 tablespoons larch or mixed
blossom honey

250 g/8 oz cherry stalks

Method:

Roast the acorns in a preheated oven, 180°C (350°F), Gas Mark 4 for 20 minutes.

Bring the water to the boil with the honey and acorns and boil for 3 minutes, then pour over the cherry stalks. Leave to infuse for 7 minutes and strain.

Chef's tip Our grandmothers would regularly use infusions of cherry stalks and were well aware of their diuretic properties. The combination of cherry stalks with acorns is more unusual. I love finding culinary uses for all nature's gifts, even the more obscure crops. I smell and taste everything, imagining possible combinations and recipes which will bring out their unique flavours.

Angelica infusion

For 1 litre/1¾ pints water

Preparation time: 5 minutes
Cooking time: 5 minutes
Infusion time: 7 minutes

Ingredients:

2 tablespoons clear honey

4 black peppercorns

4 star anise

1 lemon slice

4 cardamom seeds

6 angelica leaves

Method:

Bring the water to the boil with the honey, peppercorns, star anise, lemon and cardamom and boil for 3 minutes. Pour over the angelica leaves and leave to infuse for 7 minutes before straining.

Chef's tip Angelica, or archangelica, has many uses. Every part of this beautiful plant is aromatic. The stems are candied, the seeds are a common ingredient in pastries and liqueurs and the roots are used to flavour various liqueurs. An infusion of angelica is known to aid digestion.

Kir with truffle wine
and Luberon honey

Makes about 2 litres/3½ pints truffle wine

Preparation time: 5 minutes

Cooking time: 5 minutes

Infusion time: 2 weeks

Ingredients:

2 large truffles

500 g/1 lb clear honey

500 ml/17 fl oz white wine

Champagne

Method:

Place the truffles in the honey and leave to infuse at room temperature for 10 days.

Bring the white wine to the boil with 1.5 litres/2½ pints water. Pour over the honey and truffles, then leave to infuse for 4 days. Strain and pour into bottles.

When it is time for an aperitif, pour a little of this wine into Champagne flutes and top up with Champagne in a ratio of 1 part wine to 4 parts Champagne.

Chef's tip During the first 10 days of infusion, the truffles impart their flavour to the honey. The powerful flavour of this mushroom blends beautifully with the sweetness of the honey, producing a strong mead which makes an excellent base for cocktails.

Infusion of rose and lilac

For 1 litre/1¾ pints water

Preparation time: 5 minutes
Cooking time: 5 minutes
Infusion time: 7 minutes

Ingredients:

2 vanilla pods
1 orange slice
½ teaspoon tea
6 aromatic roses
2 lilac flowers

Method:

Bring the water to the boil with the vanilla pods, orange slice and tea and boil for 3 minutes.
Pour over the roses and lilacs and leave to infuse for 7 minutes before straining.

Chef's tip It goes without saying that you should use unsprayed flowers for this drink. You can also use dried rose petals or buds, which are available in Middle Eastern groceries or from herbalists. For me, the best aromatic rose is the eglantine or dog rose, which grows wild in Provence.

Infusion of lovage

For 1 litre/1¾ pints water

Preparation time: 5 minutes
Cooking time: 5 minutes
Infusion time: 7 minutes

Ingredients:

2 tablespoons clear honey
3 tablespoons lemon juice
½ teaspoon pepper
100 g/3½ oz lovage

Method:

Bring the water to the boil with the honey, lemon juice and pepper and boil for 3 minutes.

Pour over the lovage and leave to infuse for 7 minutes before straining.

Chef's tip Lovage is the wild ancestor of celery and can be used whenever a recipe calls for celery. Every part of the plant is aromatic. Its leaves can be used fresh or dried to flavour soups and vegetables. Their curious taste is reminiscent of celery, stock cubes and curry. The stems can be candied, while the spicy seeds are used to season pickled vegetables, marinades and fromage frais. The dried roots were used instead of pepper during the Roman period.

Spring kir with almond juice

Makes 2 litres/3½ pints almond juice

Preparation time: 10 minutes
Cooking time: 10 minutes
Infusion time: 7 days

Ingredients:

600 g/1 lb 5 oz fresh almonds
with husks
400 g/13 oz sugar
20 shelled almonds
Champagne

Method:

Process the whole almonds (with husks) with 2 litres/3½ pints water in a food processor or blender.

Pour into a jug, cover and leave to infuse at room temperature for 6–7 days, during which time the mixture will start to ferment.

On the seventh day, add the sugar. Transfer to a saucepan and bring to simmering point, then strain over the shelled almonds and leave to cool.

When it is time for an aperitif, pour a little of this juice into Champagne flutes and top up with Champagne in the ratio of 1 part juice to 4 parts Champagne.

Chef's tip This recipe requires freshly picked almonds still in their shells. To present this kir and to add a slightly sour note, I drop an unblanched almond into the glass.

Pastis with Luberon honey

Serves 4

Preparation time: 5 minutes

Cooking time: 2 minutes

Ingredients:

325 ml/11 fl oz water

2½ tablespoons clear honey

4 measures of pastis (to taste)

6 ice cubes

Method:

Bring 110 ml/3½ fl oz of the water to the boil. Pour the honey into an earthenware jug, followed by the boiling water. Add the ice cubes to cool the mixture and top up with the remaining cold water (or more, according to taste). Mix well.

Pour the pastis into glasses and top up with this mead.

Chef's tip I call this my pastis of bees because it is made with honey. The mead mixture replaces the orgeat syrup (made with almonds and sugar) usually added to pastis in Provence. I like to drink this pastis in springtime when the almond trees are flowering, since this is the fragrance of almond pastis.

Vinaigrette

Preparation time: 5 minutes
Cooking time: none

Ingredients:
3 tablespoons olive oil
4 teaspoons argan or pine nut oil
4 teaspoons groundnut oil
3 tablespoons white wine vinegar
3 tablespoons orange juice
1½ teaspoons salt
1½ teaspoons sugar
pinch of pepper

Process all the ingredients in a blender until smooth. This will produce a slightly acidic vinaigrette.

Vegetable stock

Preparation time: 20 minutes
Cooking time: 35 minutes
Standing time: 30 minutes

Ingredients:
5 carrots, chopped
2 shallots, chopped
1 garlic bulb, chopped
1 onion, chopped
1 leek, chopped
1 tomato, skinned and chopped
1 bouquet garni (parsley, fennel, bay leaf, thyme, rosemary and marjoram)
250 ml/8 fl oz white wine

Place all the vegetables in a large pan with 2 litres/3½ pints water and add the bouquet garni and wine.

Simmer for 30 minutes, then leave to stand for 30 minutes before straining. This stock can be used to dilute infusions for sauces or to thin gravy.

Chicken stock

Preparation time: 20 minutes
Cooking time: 1 hour
Standing time: 30 minutes

Ingredients:
1 kg/2 lb chicken or other poultry carcasses
150 g/5 oz carrots, chopped
75 g/3 oz celery, chopped
25 g/1 oz leek, chopped
1 onion, chopped
2 thyme sprigs
1 bay leaf

Soak the carcasses in cold water for 15 minutes, then drain.

Place all the vegetables in a large pan with the carcasses, thyme and bay leaf. Pour in 2 litres/3½ pints water and simmer for 1 hour.

Leave to stand for 30 minutes, then strain. This stock can be used as a base for numerous sauces.

Veal stock

Preparation time: 20 minutes
Cooking time: 1¼ hours
Standing time: 30 minutes

Ingredients:
20 g/¾ oz butter
1 kg/2 lb veal bones
150 g/5 oz carrots, chopped
75 g/3 oz celery, chopped
25 g/1 oz leek, chopped
1 onion, chopped
6 tomatoes, skinned and chopped
2 thyme sprigs
1 bay leaf
20 g/¾ oz plain flour
100 ml/3½ fl oz port
100 ml/3½ fl oz red wine

Melt the butter in a large pan and brown the veal bones.

Add the vegetables, thyme and bay leaf. Cook for 5 minutes, then sprinkle with flour and stir over a low heat until the flour is lightly coloured. Pour in the port, followed by the wine and bring to simmering point.

Add 2 litres/3½ pints water and bring to the boil.

Skim with a ladle and simmer for 1 hour, occasionally skimming the surface. Leave to stand for 30 minutes before straining. Like the chicken stock, this stock can be used as a base for sauces.

You can make a beef stock by replacing the veal bones with beef bones and meat. Beef stock is cooked for longer (3–4 hours). The procedure is the same for lamb stock, which is cooked for 2 hours.

Fish stock

Preparation time: 15 minutes
Cooking time: 55 minutes
Standing time: 30 minutes

Ingredients:
50 ml/2 fl oz oil
500 g/1 lb fish bones
50 g/2 oz leeks, chopped
50 g/2 oz onion, chopped
1 shallot, chopped
2 thyme sprigs
1 bay leaf
300 ml/½ pint white wine

Heat the oil in a large pan and brown the fish bones.

Add the vegetables, thyme and bay leaf, and cook for 5 minutes. Pour in the white wine and bring to simmering point, then add 2 litres/3½ pints water and bring to the boil.

Skim the surface using a ladle and simmer for 45 minutes. Leave to stand for 30 minutes, then strain.

Shellfish bisque

Preparation time: 30 minutes

Cooking time: 1½ hours

Ingredients:

50 ml/2 fl oz olive oil

750 g/1½ lb shellfish
(sea urchins, crabs, etc.)

50 g/2 oz carrot, chopped

1 onion, chopped

1 shallot, chopped

½ garlic bulb, chopped

¼ celery stick, cut into short lengths

1 leek, cut into short lengths

50 g/2 oz tomato, coarsely chopped

¼ orange

2 thyme sprigs, chopped

1 bay leaf, chopped

50 ml/2 fl oz Cognac

250 ml/8 fl oz white wine

1 teaspoon tomato purée

½ teaspoon sugar

1 tarragon sprig

200 ml/7 fl oz milk

25 g/1 oz butter

3 pinches of pepper

Heat the oil in a large pan and brown the shellfish.

Add all the vegetables, the quarter orange, thyme and bay leaf and cook for 5 minutes. Crush everything with a pestle or the bottom of a bottle, while continuing to cook the mixture over a medium heat.

Add the Cognac and ignite. When the flames die down, stir in the white wine to deglaze, then add the tomato purée, sugar and tarragon. Pour in 2 litres/3½ pints water and simmer for 1 hour.

Add the milk and cook for a further 10 minutes before stirring in the butter and pepper. Process the bisque in a blender and strain.

Puff pastry

Preparation time: 40 minutes

Standing time: 45 minutes

For the shortcrust pastry:

220 g/7½ oz butter, softened

2 teaspoons salt

650 g/1 lb 7 oz plain flour

3 eggs

For the puff pastry:

550 g/1 lb 3 oz plain flour

50 g/2 oz butter, melted

1 teaspoon salt

125 ml/4 fl oz white wine vinegar

100 g/3½ oz butter

First prepare the shortcrust pastry. Cream the butter with the salt. Place the flour in a bowl and make a well in the centre. Add the butter, and rub in with the fingertips until fully incorporated.

Make another well in the centre of the mixture. Break the eggs into the well and mix gradually, without over-kneading the dough. Roll into a ball and leave to stand for 30 minutes at room temperature, before rolling out into a square.

Now prepare the dough for the puff pastry. Mix together 500 g/1 lb of the flour, 200 ml/7 fl oz water, the melted butter, salt and vinegar. Knead well. Roll into a ball, roll out the mixture into a square and leave to stand for 15 minutes.

Roll out the puff pastry dough on a floured surface to a thickness of 1 cm/ ½ inch. Place the shortcrust pastry and the remaining butter in the centre. Fold over the puff pastry dough and roll out again to a thickness of 1 cm/½ inch. Repeat this step twice more.

Keep this dough in the refrigerator, wrapped in clingfilm, until required.

Chef's tip This pastry is a combination of shortcrust pastry and puff pastry, and offers the advantages of both. While it has more body than ordinary puff pastry (which is folded over more times and encloses only butter), it does not rise so much during cooking. However it is crustier than traditional shortcrust pastry.

Contents

Vegetables

Goat's cheese and bread

Desserts

Vinegars

Aperitifs and infusions

Basic recipes

Index of recipes

Édouard owes his generosity, high standards and professionalism to his mother Claude.

Acknowledgements

To my grandmother Raymonde, my grandfather Yvon, my mother Claude and to François, my lifelong supporters.

To my great grandmother, Charlotte.

For giving me an education and passing on their rural values.

To Isa of the mountains…

To Adrien, my magician in the garden and all the team at the Moulin at Lourmarin.

To Colette Alamel, my friend and neighbour.

To my teachers, suppliers and all the villagers of Lourmarin.

To all the team at Hachette, Brigitte, Jacques, Catherine, Dune, Anne, Carole and Stephen.

To Peter Mayle, adoptive resident of Lourmarin and fellow lover of Korthals griffons.

To Jean-Jacques, my companion and guardian angel.

To all of you, thank you, from the bottom of my heart.

Bibliography

For additional information regarding the plants mentioned in this book,
here is a non-exhaustive list of reference works.

Blamey, Marjorie and Grey-Wilson, Christopher, *Collins Mediterranean Wild Flowers*, Collins, 2001

Coombes, Allen J., *Trees (DK Handbooks)*, Dorling Kindersley, 2000

Burnie, David, *Flowers of the Mediterranean (DK Handbooks)*, Dorling Kindersley, 2000

Grey-Wilson, Christopher, *Wild Flowers of Britain and Northwest Europe (DK Handbooks)*, Dorling Kindersley, 2000

Phillips, Roger, *Mediterranean Wild Flowers (Roger Phillips Guides)*, Elm Tree Books, 1988

Polunin, Oleg and Huxley, Anthony, *Flowers of the Mediterranean*, Chatto and Windus, 1990

Veyrat, Marc, *Herbier Gourmand*, Hachette Pratique, 1997